TIRESIAS

TIRESIAS

THE COLLECTED POEMS OF

LELAND HICKMAN

Edited by **STEPHEN MOTIKA**

Preface by **DENNIS PHILLIPS**

Afterword by **BILL MOHR**

NIGHTBOAT BOOKS
Callicoon, NY

OTIS BOOKS/SEISMICITY EDITIONS
Los Angeles

Cover art: "View of Beverly Hills, from Blue Heights" by Scott B. Davis, 2004. Courtesy of the artist. http://www.scottbdavis.com

Frontispiece: undated photo of Leland Hickman by Rod Bradley. Courtesy of the artist.

Interior and cover design: typeslowly [cjmattison@gmail.com]

Library of Congress Cataloging-in-Publication Data:

Hickman, Leland.
Tiresias : the collected poems of Leland Hickman / edited by Stephen Motika ; preface by Dennis Phillips ; afterword by Bill Mohr.
p. cm.
Includes bibliographical references and index.
ISBN 978-0-9822645-1-5 (pbk. : alk. paper)
I. Motika, Stephen, 1977- II. Title.
PS3558.I2294T57 2009
811'.54--dc22
2009040480

Distributed by University Press of New England
One Court Street
Lebanon, NH 03766
www.upne.com

Nightboat Books
Callicoon, NY
www.nightboat.org

Otis Books/Seismicity Editions
Los Angeles
www.otis.edu

Table of Contents

Editor's Note and Acknowledgments

Leland Hickman was many things. He was an actor. He was an editor. He was also a poet. This book collects all the contents published in his two books: *Tiresias I:9:B: Great Slave Lake Suite* (1980), commonly referred to as *Great Slave Lake Suite*, and *Lee Sr Falls to the Floor* (1991), as well as previously uncollected and unpublished poems. I've chosen to present these poems in chronological order, although this order is approximate at best since Hickman didn't date all his manuscripts. Furthermore, many of his poems exist in multiple drafts, so it's difficult to pinpoint the exact date of completion, much less it's inception. The first poem in this book, "Call for a New Creation," was written while Hickman was a student at the University of California, Berkeley, in the mid-fifties and published in *Occident*, the university's literary magazine and has not been reprinted before now. The three longs pieces that comprise "Unpublished Early Poems" and the two fragments in "Unpublished Tiresias" have never been published and were discovered in Hickman's papers in the Archive for New Poetry at the Mandeville Special Collections at the Geisel Library at the University of California, San Diego. I honored Hickman's punctuation and notations as closely as was possible. For all other material, I followed the format of the poems in their first publication.

I discovered Hickman's work through conversations with Bill Mohr, who has done more than anyone else to bring Hickman's poetry out into the world. Now, nearly two decades after Hickman's death, Mohr is still an advocate for Hickman's poetry. He generously shared his extensive knowledge of Hickman's life and work with me and has been invaluable in the completion of this edition. I must also thank Paul Vangelisti at Otis College for insisting on the value of Hickman's work and for agreeing to co-publish this volume. Lynda Claassen, at the Special Collections Library at the University of California, San Diego; Martin Nakell, publisher of *Lee Sr Falls to the Floor*; Hickman's brother, Cliff, and sister, Nancy, have been all been supportive of this project. Thanks to Dennis Phillips for writing the preface to this book. I'm grateful to Steve Evans, Benjamin Friedlander, and Jennifer Moxley for granting me the opportunity to speak about Hickman at the National Poetry Foundation's conference on The Poetry of the 1970s at the University of Maine in June 2008. Thanks also to Julia Alter, Rod Bradley, Scott B. Davis, Clayton Eshleman, Kathleen Fraser, Photios Giovanis, Kevin Killian, Christopher Mattison, Libby Motika, and Aaron Shurin.

Leland Hickman: Against Taxonomies

BY DENNIS PHILLIPS

There may come a time when our cultural provincialisms will be seen with a wider lens. In the world of poetry, what urgently seemed the product of one or another region, of this or that school of thought or MFA program or social network or journal, will be seen as threads of a whole fabric, American perhaps, perhaps European. That we haven't yet arrived at that moment does nothing if not cement our notions of boundaries, categories, organizations, and the specificities, but also the limitations that go with them.

Leland Hickman would have none of that, at least not when it came to poetry.[1] In his work as editor and in his vocation as poet, he resisted such limitations, he rejected orthodox taxonomies.

The expansive fields of interest that fed Hickman's poetry are apparent by looking at his development as an editor. Beginning his stint as the poetry editor of *Bachy*, the journal published by Papa Bach Paperbacks, one of the now-lost literary bookstores of Los Angeles, Hickman basically continued the tradition of focusing on local writers that he inherited as he assumed the editorial reins for *Bachy*'s last several issues. But even so, he was interested in expanding the kinds of poetries he would publish there and, perhaps, the notions of poetry's potential for his readers. When the bookstore folded the magazine in 1981—not too long before the store itself closed—Hickman had not had his fill of editing literary journals. He seems to have seen an avenue for his creative and intellectual energies that he could play out on a national and international scale, and which he may have felt to be an external counter-balance to his intensely internal poetic work.

Soon after the folding of *Bachy*, Hickman teamed up with poet and translator Paul Vangelisti to found *Boxcar*, a "Journal of the Arts," that drew on both Vangelisti's experience co-editing the seminal and distinctly international journal *Invisible City*, and Hickman's editorial work on *Bachy*. In 1983 the only two issues of *Boxcar* came out.[2] Undeterred, and perhaps grateful to find the excuse to work alone—collaboration was not his strong suit—in 1985 Hickman brought out the first issue of his landmark journal *Temblor*, which bore witness to his vast poetic research.

The 10th and final issue of *Temblor*, which came out in 1989, ends with a comprehensive index that documents Hickman's eclectic editorial reach. Of its many remarkable attributes, *Temblor* succeeded in placing in the hands of a vast and often unrelated group of American and international poets the work of their fellow travelers that they may easily have missed. If that could be said of other journals or anthologies, few can claim to have done so with the thoroughness and commitment to broadening the view of contemporary poetry that *Temblor* did, and very few can claim the gravity that *Temblor* created, or to have been a venue for such multifarious energy.

What may not have been apparent, though, was that Hickman's practice as a poet drove his work as editor/publisher. What slipped too easily from the awareness of the poets and other readers for whom his editorial work was of great importance, was the remarkable body of poetry that Leland Hickman had written. What was never apparent to those who knew only *Temblor*, was that a poet of great emotional and intellectual power made one endeavor possible because of his dedication to and, possibly, his retreat from the other.

The volume you are holding in your hands represents Leland Hickman's complete poetic production, and his greatest legacy. There were those, during the *Temblor* days, who praised the journal but dismissed the editor's own poetry.[3] Some said the work was too autobiographical, others that the homosexuality was too guilt-ridden. Some said the language was too dense, others that it was overly dramatic. But those voices fade as time allows Hickman's poetry to stand away from temporary issues, from issues of no importance to the work he made. Hickman's work also presents an interesting problem for those who would categorize it.

From its title, its length, and its complex arrangement,[4] *Great Slave Lake Suite*—the bulk of Hickman's mature work—decidedly follows a High Modernist tradition. Yet he seems to have jettisoned the modernist tendency to "impersonalize"[5] the poetic work by using autobiography as the core of the poem. Though the work is very personal, by dimension and mythic ambition, it's not confessional. There is a sweeping narrative, but the poem's not narrative in any conventional sense. And there is a dense and shifting lyricism, symphonic in its scope, that might seem Romantic were it not for the thoroughly contemporary dissonance that Hickman deploys to challenge the very musicality that drives the work.

I once heard Hickman respond to a *Temblor* reader's challenge that the journal was too focused on "Language" poetry.[6] Rather than engage in a mathematical argument (how many poets self-identified with that group were included versus all the others) Hickman asked the reader to explain to him what "Language" poetry was. Each time the reader gave a definition, Hickman countered with another "Language Poet" who didn't fit the definition. In one quick conversation, Hickman defined a major tenet of his poetics, forced a reader to a less category-driven way of approaching poetry, and demolished the notion that, although there were those who were called Language Poets, there really wasn't anything that could be identified as "Language Poetry." Turning to me when the reader had left, Hickman said that he saw himself as a scientist, by which I took him to mean that his research led him to his editorial and poetic work; that he didn't begin with a conclusion and then back fill with his writing; that experience in life, in writing, in editing, in reading were the vectors that led to his work; that he applied his reading, his writing, his living—enhanced by his eidetic memory—to the projects he undertook, and insisted that the results be self-defining.

His oeuvre, as intense and concentrated as any of the 20th century, was also relatively small. Hickman, who made his living for the last decade of his life as a typesetter, devoted nights and weekends to every aspect of *Temblor*.[7] Perhaps the energy that he spent editing his journal drained Hickman of the stamina demanded by the composition of his poetry.[8] Perhaps, had he lived longer—he died in 1991 at the age of 56—his work on *Tiresias*[9] may have continued. Perhaps he meant the work to be unfinished; Hickman was strategic enough to have planned such a move.

Among the many strengths of Hickman's poetry is a magnitude of tone that might be described as epic but for its deeply introspective intent. It might easily be described as dramatic, but there's danger in that because the work's particular type of drama—a quality that helps to push it out of any expected category or school—is ingrained in its brooding, prophetic musicality, not in sentimental histrionics. What may well be the defining trait of Hickman's work is that it draws deeply from the ritualistic, dithyrambic culture out of which emerged the ambi-gendered figure of Tiresias and the public nature of the personal dilemmas he both endured and was called on to inform. That cultural spring—Hickman's Tilphussa[10]—is the lens through which the drama that characterizes the "Great Slave Lake Suite," for example, might be viewed.

Hickman's sense of drama was no doubt influenced by his early training as an actor. As any who saw him read could attest, he had a fine sense of theatricality. It was not a hand wringing, jugular popping kind of theatricality, but a seething control of tempo, an explosive restraint, a well-honed sense of audience.

When I think of that aspect of Hickman's skill set, I remember one event in particular that somehow encapsulates so much of what was surprising about him.

One evening while having dinner with Hickman and his longtime partner, the character actor Charles Macaulay, I mentioned that I would soon be teaching a Shakespeare course. My hosts' eyes lit up with curiosity about which plays I'd be covering. With some disappointment, Charles asked me why I wasn't going to use *Henry V*. When I said that I didn't really care for that play, Charles leaned in towards me and with almost a whisper said, "Lee once did a one-man show of Henry Five." Hoping to end the discussion, I turned to Lee: "If you'll do that for my class, I'd be happy to teach the play." He took a breath and with a pained expression agreed.

A couple of weeks before he was scheduled to visit my class, Lee called me wanting to know exactly how long the session would last and what the physical layout of the room was. When I asked him what he was planning, "You'll see," was all I got.

On the evening of his presentation, he arrived with an enormous edition of the collected plays that looked as if it had come from a prop house. In the very small classroom, he instructed us to push the seminar table against the wall, which freed up some space in the center. The students and I sat around the three sides of the table facing the single chair Lee had placed in the middle of his improvised stage.

After we had settled, he let the silence expand for a moment, before, seated in his chair, he opened the huge tome and began to read the prologue. When he finished it he clapped the book shut, set it on the floor beside the chair, stood up and began performing. He acted in full dimension each of the characters—including the princess Katherine, in French and in falsetto—moving around the room, at times bringing his face right up to one of the student's, at times retiring to the far corners of the small space.

When I glanced over at my students to see how they were responding to this singular event, I was amazed to see a dozen usually tired and semi-interested students riveted to, mouths agape at Lee's literally breathtaking performance. For two hours, he was flawless. There was never an unintended pause, never a miscue or flubbed line, never a loss of focus. Not only was it one of the most extraordinary theatrical performances I had ever seen, anywhere, it also seemed to me, in an oblique way, the embodiment of Lee Hickman as a poet: his command of language in service to an encyclopedic and photographic memory, his masterful use of the dynamics of language, his skill at extracting a wellspring of humanity from the complex strains of language, his willingness to risk.

Much more could be said of Leland Hickman, as "figure," as a dynamic component of an often invisible poetry community, as a refined and refining force in American poetry. Mostly, though, his importance rests in the pages that follow. So, as prelude, in closing, in opening, a stanza from Hickman's last poem, "He Who Delights in Signs:"

angerly glad flung, mad by infected
feastings, starkt as to dread, dasht to last
wishes, cobwebby viral word blood temblor this
stumbler in naked elision, enjambments stunned, at alarm's
distance, syllable hell in a panic deathwell toxic bittersweet sleep of who drink thee

Notes

[1] When Lee Hickman began his editorial work in the late 1970s, he was immediately subjected to the complex weave of specialized concerns that replicated in one location the riven world of American poetry as it existed at the dawning of the Age of Ronald Reagan. As Hickman's work continued, the labels shifted and particular concerns morphed into others, but the tendency to divide and trench in remained a constant feature of a literary terrain that he categorically rejected.

[2] The last issue of *Bachy* had taken a note-worthy turn toward national and international poetry. The collaboration between Hickman and Vangelisti logically extends Hickman's new-found editorial interests with Vangelisti's well-established commitment to creating a forum for international thinking and writing.

[3] Hickman never published his own work in *Temblor*.

[4] For example, the full title of *Great Slave Lake Suite*, *Tiresias I:9:B: Great Slave Lake Suite*, suggests a grand and complex form.

[5] E.g. T.S. Eliot's essay "Tradition and the Individual Talent."

[6] An absurd notion given the broad and unbiased combination of poetic points-of-view in each issue of *Temblor*.

[7] As far as I know, *Temblor* was a complete one-man show. Every aspect, from typesetting and design, to soliciting and editing the contents, to managing subscriptions and searching for money were handled by Hickman alone.

[8] As one whom Hickman often published, I can bear witness to the rigor with which he approached his duties. Never did I submit a poem or series of poems to him that did not undergo his fine-tuned scrutiny. There was never any consideration given to friendship or hurt feelings. Hickman fired away with an acuity that has remained unmatched. Those encounters were not always pleasant. They were, however, more than productive, they were formative.

[9] As alluded to before, *Tiresias* is the name of his major project; *Great Slave Lake Suite*, a section of *Tiresias*, was the most fully realized component of the whole.

[10] "Tilphussa, or Telphousa: spring near Sphinx Mountain, from which Tiresias prophesied he would drink and then die." Author's note at the end of Hickman's last addition to *Tiresias*.

EARLY POEMS

Call for a New Creation
(Berkeley or Anywhere)

Refusing to thank you for this
handful of
        thorns
or sit apart like a syphilitic
nervously pretending a
        calm cognizance
of your dumb hoots and toots,
WHAT I DEMAND IS THE DRAMATIC

stick to split basilisks
        from bankrupt air
Tiresias stick, Tiresias female
to coil the retinae of fatalities
on a stretched canvas, and utter
        and wholly ghost
false makings, still movements, and entities
NON-EXISTENTLY SNAKED BETWEEN
        EYE AND EYE

Do all our babes got blind eyes?
Eye, spy, and woman-become, die and
        become snake and
outshoot sperm like a Van Gogh
landscape, or Hopkins inscape, and
        onlooker, snake-
struck, will die, gain, be whole, and not
NOT WORTH SHAKING A STICK AT

Onlookers, lively, dying and bearing
        then act, have
action thrust into his-her malewombs,
return, delivered most whole therefrom,
        dying, and bearing
new and unblind eyes. Be then suicidal:
Die some, pound a snake with a stick:
CREATE THESE PEOPLE, BE FOR
        THEM FERTILE

And, onlookers, you dumb hooters
and tooters, begin
to find out where your mothers are—when I
eye you, when I
eye you, I mean to remove your heads:
my glance is two insanities, filled
with a blue hiss, blowing your direction—
WHISPER WISHWELLS TO ALL YOUR
VANITIES.
ONLOOKERS, LIVELY, DYING AND
BEARING, NOW ACT!

.:

Anaximander

In the final nites of the Infinite,
when out of the sleeping sea,
                the prickly-skinned crawl,
generation will dry their days
And after their skins
                break off them,
they will live for a little while

In the final nites of the Infinite,
wherefrom all things conceivable spring,
the fish will change
                into the man
the bear will change
                into the man
the spider, mouse, antelope
all living things
                will change
into the prickly skin of man,
there to live for a little while
And the sun will raise new vapors
lifted by the Infinite
                into new living things
thrust into the sleeping sea
to float there,
                until their final nite
But what shall we do,
                Diogenes,
when the wheel refuses to turn again,
when all of our stars are stopped up,
and when finally the sea
                is completely dry?

[1956]

Charles, viewed in the silver

Charles, viewed in the silver,
whose days attend his wants
somnambulistic nurses
masculine and hauntingly polite
sits quietly reading
Harley Granville-Barker, the melancholy Dane,
holds up the skull of Yorick
(the old dog inside him lies so still
mourning the death of the family
and the burning down of the house)
not knowing anyone sees.

    Far away in the ear of the ocean
    his grandmother's bones tell secrets.

Charles, young and cognizant,
knows death comes in flashes
utterances of mystics
wild-eyed and furtive
yet worships his grandmother's bones,
the counterfeit presentment of kings
and other images sparked in a dark ravine
(the falcon tethered to his pulse
hooded, almost dead
as patient as the dead)
when no one is looking.

    Far away in the ear of the ocean
    his sons tell tales as they wait.

[1962]

Work On What Has Been Spoiled

Dry low tough hills
tumbleweed rolling
caught in a windy fence
Who makes it roll
The wind
We whirl in hot tough wind
laughing, inside our heads
tumbleweeds
tossed in a windy dance

Burrs in bare feet
Run precariously
through vacant lots
to play with Bob and Billy

Kecksies, wild seeds,
in t-shirt wilderness
Bury me alive naked
Their mother called them in
But they did not go
They stared at me
Curious, strange me
Who are you, Sonny
We want to play good
(Play nasty)
(Play nasty)
Their mother called them in
They did not go
Smiled into the air at
a loss at a loss at a loss
Come on, shovel dirt on me
Breathing dust in bare
mind, in a tough wind

Whispered twisted syllables
Nebraska, Arkansas, Ireland
brooding behind us as we slept
Nebraska, Arkansas, Ireland

picked up our dropped words
hid them for our dreams
salvaged in secret secret falsities,
fears, secreting nightmares
out of old daylights, brewing
poison with stunted roots of years

Time in the San Joaquin
to be alone
No friends
President Roosevelt suddenly stopped
talking to me
Daddy might go to Europe
The Japanese would come and get us
In the low hot tough hills
tumbleweed dust burrs
vacant lots vacant friends

The lean-to porch on the shack
nailed into my mind
My father hammered on the house
in a hurry in a hurry
In Japan people burned

Fried rabbit fried heart
Humming in anemic voice
Mother in the kitchen
ironing
by the pulldown table
hooked against the wall
no room
Ration stew leafy kale
Humming in pale lassitude
Mother in the kitchen
Fried rabbit fried heart

Silent, daddy in the warplant
Silent, daddy in the Model T
Silent, daddy in the muddy drive
and the magenta car
roast black
burned exploded in the night

Smoking daddy
always the cause
Curse you

Lake Street asphalt melted
in the sparkling heat
then the long weeds   the uncut grass
ruffling up to the shack
the six castor-bean trees
oilcloth-leaved, crimson-thistled, heavy
flabbergasted along the gashed driveway's
two sun-dried ruts
neglected from idleness
deep from the rains   weight of duties
hungry bites by the old car
out of the earth to make it to the shack
erected by my father out of lack
Covered the roof with black
tarpaper

Nebraska, Ireand, Arkansas
beneath that thin yellow tree
backyard sour plum
gummy pits barbed in bare feet
pulp oozes   between toes
Boards on boxes make a counter
play restaurant,
sell plums and mashes bananas
to the absent children
who live across the vacant lots
under the long blue, and clouds
in the sparkling plum-strewn heat

Nebraska, Ireland, Arkansas
sprouted weeds
in the drought of anxious eyes
Arkansas, Nebraska
Ireland (Mother humming anemic voice)
headaches in the heat   in the rain I
see her, dark-haired
wearing a blue bathrobe
standing still on the planks that cover mud

9

the way to the outhouse
in the storm   holding her
hands to her face
screaming   screaming
for nothing

[1964]

Further Work On What Has Been Spoiled

I.

Guilt lays no eggs, its young
slide from its mouth full-grown
This guilt that curls around
my fingers make no sound
as it bleeds them, and around
my feet, and wound along
my gnarled bitten tongue,
splits its slimy lips
dropping down each lung
its squeezed-out hungry young
that crawl into my words and cling
like vibrant dung; the throng
of rots that sleep across my lids
clot my brain   Guilt that feeds
on guilt is never hungry long.
   And decay has no ending.

II.

Moments in my mind:
maggots in a carcass
putrid in sun. Air so thick.
Memories in silent gasps
Evaporate. Mother and Father.
Sister. Brothers. Friends.
Lovers who kissed my sickness
(and so the wise were conned)
Teachers, even Tiresias my whisperer,
who lured me into hell with them.
Tiresias spirit/Tiresias female
who stirred me with his stick
when I was batter in a bowl
uncaked yet, prophesying
neither chaos nor decay,
   nor cities I'd enter.

11

III.

Or perhaps I am pisswater in a pool
in some beast-traveled street at night
with the moon's reflection on my scum.
Even the moon cannot escape me
or else does not reject me.

It shines upon stagnation as a friend.

The sun will be my end.

[1964]

Lee Sr Falls to the Floor

his breathing unthrobs

Rerun that   The fumes
tremble in the terrifying heat
Lee Sr falls to the floor

Rerun that   Lee Sr crumples
angular on linoleum
gasps in the kitchen glare

Rerun   Lee Sr falls down
in jockey shorts   A wooden
chair topples on its side   smacks
the floor   back goes
his balding head   clawed
by ache

                    Rerun the gasp

Rerun these inching thru
instantaneous reruns with
a feel to the eyes of
unfocused imagery

Rerun that   Lee Sr crumples.
dead. In the bed   down
the halflit hall
his greyveined mistress
sleeps out of life whose
fleshings creamed his dark.
The boy her grandson falls
in the hallway   hands gripped
to the urgent splitting of
time away   his pajamas
drenched with the wet
of fire quenching fire   They're
dead   and so the fumes
have no more purpose   no
effect   effected

by agents out of time
who do not know the job is
done   who never despair
never tire   never quit

Gasp in the kitchen's glare
In the halflit sweating hall
the deadly fumes   Speak from eyes
ears taste touch gut:

                                    Rerun all

this: the fumes rise
as nearsighted Clifford
peers thru deathsprinkled glass
raps   shatters the glass
trembling at the hot
voom of decayed breath
And walks thru the dark
living room rapidly   no
rerun that   inches thru
the black toward the
flame of the heater   no
paralyzed   coughs   waits.
afraid to move utterly.
toward the light from the hall.
slashed across the floor.
squinting Clifford.
afraid to move utterly.

Rerun! Instantaneously
dashes toward the light
sees peripherally someone still
in a shadowed bed
down the lungdamp hall—
stilled creamdark fleshings
whose images fumed and flamed—
hurries thru the hall over
the dead boy peers
thru the kitchen's glare   sees
one bare foot gelid blue.

'I am a tiny child'
whimper the words in him
as the floor slides back
as the boy dies
whose death it is
as he sweats for the warm
still halfseen someone.

      We take a greyhound bus,
      we run to an angry dad.

      Rerun that   We go home

         Cliff
stoops to lift the broken
chair and slumps down staring
at a hole in the brown linoleum, near
his father's bent bare
unfocused image
fixed in fleshings as
creamy blue and as stiff as
two days dead and never before
beaded with sweat like this final sweat

And now rerun
the gasp the ache the urgent
splitting the stumbling fall
the toppling chair the
quitting the rapping the
rapping the breaking glass and
the personages as
flickering stills the
personages muffled   I
hang up   I tell my brother John   We board
a greyhound bus   We
go home   holding our
breaths in fear
that our breaths will vanish
claimed by an angry god

No, rerun that We go home:
We just / go home.

                  [1965]

UNPUBLISHED EARLY POEMS

Virgo I

Virgo is visited
demons of dark he
sees also alone
bits of beauty.

Long is
to and fro time
the hungry cat's
eyes   indecipherable
codes in corner's
unpacked boxes of books,
or a car slows on the corner/
    mouths see me
looking   walking along.

Tasted tho
savorless pro/
viding nourishment
Virgo seeking
provisions of it.

Without it, is
it lost: laughter?
Harvest of her
breast at birth
or births before.
Details of attrition
dropping after.
Virgo.

        Void or
Wyrd or Word
where the power is/
was/   wide awake
not to prey and peer for
it   is forlornness
white walls without
floor   foreheard
ceiling lightbulb

burnt out   0

Jewels gems   rubies
diamonds sapphires followed
me   My father found in
it the Virgo stone   we
two 13
days dividing us   now
loose on a little bone
deep in a hill.

Virgo Two

On the day of my birth
a famous poet's daughter
set herself on fire
In the flames she saw
her father's ruddy face

Rubedo of frenzy flows
from the charred chalice.

Who sees in this event
the burning of the whole world
    appropriation of the lost
        power in holocaust
protects his creation

Rubedo of frenzy flows
from the charred chalice.

The end of identity
was transmutation once.
The goal of our energy
lies in fake stasis:
in destruction utterly
        to be destroyed

The poet's face in flames
a sinless penance

Who in this dis-use
in the lack of connection
    between the rite enacted
    and loss of what's meant
sees pus of his disease
        protects creation

Only a sinless penance
the poets' gaze thru flames.

She gave her mind to fire
the days of my mind's entrance
Magicians of the world
grimace and drink smoke
raising the charred chalice.
Who sees this mindless penance

sees no poet in the blaze
no stone from extinction.

Virgo III

I think of my birthday because
Irene casts horoscopes   Irene
She asks me the time of my birth
I'll write to mother   Irene
Suddenly she's in the office and
says I want your birth date   Irene
whose hands tremble   whose voice
is an unaware oracle   Irene
comes into my office only a few times
each week.

When I'm with her
the elevator
the coffee stand
standing by grey desks

there is her fragility
and long dark hair
shall I mention her
eyes
she breathes through a little nose and half-open mouth
Then I want to fill my whole mouth with her.

I'm Sagittarius she says sagely
as though I could not understand
But my husband hates astrology.
Bad planets hang in the air
dripping malevolent influence of which
I know I have always been aware.
She wears a ring. She is a little thing.
She is someone who casts horoscopes.

Virgo Four

Poetry.
Levertov: the Olga Poems.
When faces speak
teeth showing
  nourishment from what
  silences?
teeth bared
  jaws biting
off what how do you do?

In the constructed
               thing
to make it sing like
two common sets of cavities
  nourishing three silences

from form strictly formed from
the jaw-set and tongue's length
and geometries of utterance

over the noises
           machinery
muscles bracketed by tools
automobiles
         people laughing in them
rushing air cooling
          to move into
such collisions of heat
in profound beat
time to buildings rising
  pillars of grit
high over heads from
  beneath sore feet

for the o the need
the need
need
   need
      the

taut twist of it to say
it
   in a construction stiff
with glass cement plastic steel
tough and the symbols if symbols
still not wisdoms wrenching away;
        falling from themselves;
          like skyscrapers;
sighing crashing down;
killing cars and the poets in them.

Poetry.
Levertov: the Olga Poems.
The groceryman at Gristede's
the cabdriver   hand on cock
the cleaner's clean deliverer, young
with sleek black hair and
     dancer's   legs
thoughts in the brain of the city
struggling   kicking up their legs
    Saturdays and birthdays
instead of kicking out. as helpless
                as verse.

To sprout my country or anyone's Olga
in their ears and in their voices
free it back to me thus nothing personal/
Personal nothing:

By ear
     he sd
Of course but.

Levertov: the Olga Poems.
8,000,000 grieving
in their way/ with
no awareness as to why.

And Mencius:
   If we wish to know
whether anyone is
   superior or not

we need only observe
    what parts of his being
he regards as especially
    important—

The buildings rise.
Then haggard from
lost purposes
they are jarred
by our metal gods
gnawing their entrails
              and

Inhabitants
Openly
        with angry screeches   grunts
disparate/not suiting/no con/
nection to
professed intents

O Ear is full and mouth
is full, jaws set to
belie and in lying
forget.

The strictest attention
Mencius
by eye
refutes coherence
to strictest attention
by ear.

Alone, in my ear.

Virgo Five

This day I write of
ended with a poem in
a Greek restaurant because
I'd ceased to read   It
came 'by ear'   I call it
Marriage Chant: Forehead and Sternum
and what it says I dreamt
last weekend, ignorant
of course of its meaning but
now that I know
who's to hear?

The Creative works
sublime success.

In deepest dungeons.
Even alchemists—
but time and still
time they're under/
stood bit by bit.
I will not think of it.
Ginny on the telephone
said it was good   I wrote
it over, perfecting
ear and tried to sleep—
couldn't in its wake.

The Creative works
sublime success.

Ginny's psychic dreams:
'veridical' Lionel fears to
call it, of the bus
driver let his bus
crash, because the bus
driver's name was his boss'
name, unknown to her, and thinks
his future must be disastrous.
The Virgo stone (in earth)

Irene will (may) read or
else the flesh burnt in flames.

The Creative works
sublime success.

Difficulty in the mind
difficulty in the heart
or in stars the difficulty
in voice ear in this city
in touch of the type/
writer even, even in
my ear's eye's focus/ that
there is still alive now not
one soul knows that he/she
sees with me in this event
the burning of the whole world.

But the Creative
works sublime success.

Virgo Six

& beneath the bedclothes coil
iambs of mutable sleep
I am if I am if I am if
hisses thru pillows snake confesses
secrecies 'All, therefore, that has
been confessed by me consists of
fragments of a great confession;
and this little book is an attempt
which I have ventured on to render
it complete': In Goethe's Autobio.
Waking   the lightshits on that Vir/
go purifying evolution's
messages in Rome   Today
(round & round & no one knows)
Irene says Lee my damned ephemeris
left you out   I tried to start
from 33 but that went nowhere
My husband he came home so I
put all my playthings away they
make him livid   (her only
infidelity   Thank you
Irene I'll never tell)   In
this office is another Virgo
Shelly whose sons & husband
thank her stars/She also is
adept in starwords/promises
as soon as mother writes   to
find the heaven synchronous to
what has & will evolve
Revolve   Evolve   Cyclic &
linear unite, Pere Teilhard
de Chardin? So stars escape
the wheel infits real rut
the dying holding together
the delivered falling apart?
Is separate/is isolate/is odd
is God's if then, & wild self
gift on any deathday, look
into my chart: those planets

are dead & others will die,
for is it both if/time end/
ing and the begins of it
in fresh line reconnecting
connecting connecting connect/
ing while leaves stir irritably
in the tree of disturbance.

Virgo Seven

With the palm of my hand, if
after wiping its sweat off, if
with the lust of my hand I
had touched   thrust my tentacle
past the crowd and felt there
proud is his beige tight
slacks   his ass   not cock   If I
break down   If I'd cried out to
him   in a trapped seamonster's
roar bellowing it: Here it
is/the face you'll grow/the heart
you'll forever be able to die by/and for

your sputum your spit   a soft
sink   No simply no
                            it was his

well-exhibited buttocks
No it was that naïve haircut
the slash of summersharp hook of
him in my fish eyes   the
privateness of his (blue) sweater
which he must have left at home
in the bureau next to his older
brother's cardigan   he must
live in Brooklyn   no, he
leapt the stairs; in; front;
of me in sunlight   with dust
on his black suede shoes   If
I had or could pet those shapes
of illusionary always
young   would I seem too far
gone   would I lick his fat

            shoes also?

Virgo Eight

Earlier, on the subway, read
Ernest Sandeen's Day in June

in which he speaks of maple
leaves that line the diverse

by dancing in the wind totally
How out of the fact of

shimmering   shimmering is all
and a way of life is extracted

A few leaves dance in disturbance
then the entire corps de ballet.

In one of those firm moments
are no face or ties   everything

is shoes and indefinite color
1,000 orchestrated breathings

of people waiting   holding on
morning and evening and morning

sounds in the unlit tunnel
as green sun in the mind

shimmers   a few shattered
primary glitterings then the roar

as trains stops then chattering
all the leaves in excitation

together   A sense of something
winding blindly in the dark

and coming up fresh   Unfirm
diffuse   the connections   unfixed.

Connecting center to eccentric
yet is a severing   when leaf fall

means a new thing   Dogma in a
breeze and the poem about it

a fixing of beginning   the sign
of shimmer is the poem's

juxtapositions. Upstairs where
headlines scream for God's sake.

Virgo Nine

In this world green means go
red stops you   little girls
in white's hue plural are pure
In this world, translucent
noncolor has no definition
its nothing means all
And after the subways
and after the subways of today
a cold hint of that nonlight

Dusk   A published poet
lives nearby   walking home from
work   dark blue suit and tie
Could he smell my wordless book
and yearning on my breath?
Not for your body, or love
Not after the subways of today:
it's you nonlight, its cold look
attracts me, for my ambition

But you, you're not really nonlight
you, you're my scecret message, my
symbol rushing thru the twilight
you're line consonant and vowel
hinting of apotheosis
only in my hope   Ignored
and after the subways of today
shy, following distantly
burning for delusive nonlight

Crossed against the red stoplight
then you entered Prima's Grocery
then again crossed but at green
next seen disappearing thru
a door on Second Avenue   Covertor
leaning on a parking meter   re/
flected in a single smashed window
of an empty tenement   What's this?
Am I a dog that sniffs at doors

or cat that leaps at invisible
inferior mice? Green is go
Subways signal red threats
Wherever the nonlight the saint/
light is there is not stealth
in giving death up like wealth

(Deviating from the path
 to seek nourishment from the hill
 Continuing to do this brings misfortune)

Years ago, at a grim cocktail
party, I was young you wouldn't
remember, you said to me Salinger
is walking a perilous path thru his
words, so close to the edge of
his own life   And you shook your blond head

   .....

in the middle of night time where is
the Bliss Goddess of the East Village?

o if she has measles I hope she won't die

Virgo Ten

Sullivan Street late afternoon Italian teenagers during the early
       hours of the St. Anthony Street Festival watch the deaths
       of fires in bottles fires they stuff into bottles to
       watch suffocate   I stop
Beside the bottled flame this muscular boy squats exposing startling
       white tense meat where his levis gape open at the back
       quickly I strip him moaning he comes sweet I brook him
       back and forth over teethpebbles I drink the white syrupy
       rapids Ginny smiles at me she doesn't know this glare this
       glinting water of darkness surrounds surrounds
This coddling breeze through her light hair parts also the salty
       hairs on these darting skins young ungraspable so secret
Now see us we stroll as though enchanted through fleshy carnival
       Festival street our intimate smiles our calm summery talk
       smother reality it burns we know undying but unfelt
We may as well confess it we are all of us dead inside.

               Sky o glistening torsos o
               solar secretions o lights
               glare o
               soon twilight feeds
               grass to these thick chests
               to moustached throats,
               sucking grass to twisted
               eyelids tangled in
               night's roots o decay
               in the street o gleaming
               bones of the heart
               picked o sunbones o
               the birds fly up from the street,
               from our company
               circling in the sky o
               widening o
               narrowing o
               wing bellows flapping in/
               hale to the sun's torsos o
               breathing out, into
               life o acolytes of

sun o mirages of
sky o & messages o &

None dare to see

struggle of
suffocating   flame

FIRST MESSAGES:
from Gershom G. Scholem, Marshall McLuhan, William Burroughs,
Dizzy Gillespie, Hans Morgenthau, Joseph Kraft, Dag Hammarskjöld,
Douglas Cooper, Gavin Lambert, Michael O'Brien, Morton Feldman,
Wallace Stevens & Buddha.

      1.

Dragonflies
     blot out
         the sunset

Clarion/ toward annihilation:
    coats of skin,
with a very minute allowance for some star dust

Paradisiacal garments of the soul
a heap of unarranged letters
    'And Lotah's sister was Timna'
the whole day
     (As woman's trials at sin tend
      So went alas man's dirt stain),
in accordance with the names that flare.

Cadmus sowed
dragon's teeth
Sprang up armed men
Teeth
    emphatically visual
Letters/
    teeth,
      visually.

To & fro a
random
    craving for images
a page of Rimbaud
cut up & rearranged

                    I tell you boss you write it
                    and it happens
                    why if you didn't write
                    me I wouldn't be here:

Mystic scribes in the
Wrath of the Second Aeon
In the next
        a new
            Torah.

It burned down.

                                2.

                Finding chords/
                        threw a different light on

        the whole sound

Oh, music is so infinite you
only get a little bit of it

                the literal
                clothed in black
                linear organization of the letters
                nunlike tenacity

a compulsion to protect
their imaginary world
form all contact with the real one

Only poets & sages succeed
eating soup with a knife.

(Clothespins sir uh—
        Don't need any thank you
—uh I'm dying (hic)!—

                Pride of faith more
                        unforgiveable dangerous
                than pride of intellect
                a split personality
                faith "observed" & appraised
                negating the unity of
                      dying-unto-self
                "value" faith/
                        metaphysical magic
                reserved for a spiritual
                elite

                        Respect for
                        the word

Gia/
cometti
struggles &
stutters
self-torture than an adven/
ture
detached, all-penetrating eye
a humble copyist

disengage
totally form history

insubstantial record
incapable of coping

Voice of Lady Bracknell as she adds
--"and that should be a warning to us
all!"

                                        3.

The objects which support my life

trapped in the cerebral cathedral

            idea/opium
            you have integrity when
            your whole life is based
            on accumulation of ideas?

If we escape destruction
            destruction
at the hands of the logical positivists
if we cleanse the imagination
            imagine!
of the taint of the romantic

            we still face

To fidget with points of view leads always to
              new beginnings
Incessant new beginnings lead to
              sterility.

      o Death carries off
        the gathered flowers
      o Death carries off
        a man who is gathering flowers

              on the wild wind side
              of the hill, with
              the whisper soft clouds
              encircling, he
              fades into the onewordstanza, he
              becomes quiet.

SECOND MESSAGES:
from Arthur Schopenhauer, The Bahir

Homer Plato Horace & the others for thousands of years
to the disheartened with persistent fidelity

Buddha's Holy Tooth
Petrarch's house in Arqua
Tasso's supposed prison in Ferrara
Shakespeare's house in Stratford, with his chair
Goethe's house in Weimar, with its furniture
Kant's old hat the autographs
of great men these things are
gaped at with interest and awe
(Merely)
subject-matter of a poet's works
the personal circumstances
not the (living) form

        The spider's small breath
        is his web, his house, his foods
        spun forth
        his inner form
        it is his own aesthetic experience
        sparkling with various thoughts
        in the soft breeze
        after the soft
        morning rain

I was alone when I made it
I was there before thee
who could have been with me to whom
I might have confided this secret?

        Hierarchy of persons
        being difficult to descry
        hop on the back of this butterfly & see
        the tiny lights flickering in flowers
        the tiny cunts that open wisely
        to the fuck of the moon:
        hierarchy of persons: a kingdom
        of open form filled

It is
far beyond this seashore which is my body
this white sand these green shoreweeds sprouting from me
not this lucid water nor the rays of searching
that reach down down & down into the darker
& the darker realms of forms alive
past the brown past forms
into the blue dark freedom
they have not ever touched
the underneath of ocean the
underneath of underneath of oceans
underneath not even there has it yet come home.

THIRD MESSAGE:
from The Bahir, Gershom G. Scholem

it lies in the north of God
a principle called 'Evil'
it breaks forth
out of the north

it is the form of the hand
frozen on the key of the iron gate in ice
(& it has many messengers

   confuses
   men
   until they sin
   only
   until they sin

    Automobiles are in my ears
    as streaks of darkness passing
    out of the north
    by my windows
       the rain
    bounces off them
        the wet mice
    are squeezed
    out of the tires
    They are not evil
    They only sound
       evil

The form of the hand is muscular & hirsute
over my eyes & thru the blood vessels
outstanding everything is tinged

the rain is scarlet
(which falls in it)
Not an evil
   hue

    Demonization of life
    in concrete embodiment
    crude town feelings

                    admiration/
                    revulsion

    the piercings   visited by   the wrenchings
    the piercings   demons of   over & over
    over & over   bits of   the wrenchings
    the piercings   beauty   the wrenchings

    a continuance   a breach   a nothing
                a many   a one
                    or demons
                the essence

roar of sparks from the wheels in rain & thunder
gentle crickets chorale of the mechanical island

                        & dogs barking out their jazz.

FOURTH MESSAGE:
from Alan Watts

       Quesy labyrinth of my own insides
a confusion of bushes
a rotten log bearing rows of fungus
       fugues in cartilage
           counterpoint in capillaries
             rhythm in nerve
               blown & caressed
                    caressed to a passion

While in a cheap velvet coffin
a days/dead Negro in a vision
    black skin tight over bone
his lids half open
tortured & tearing the threads
there, way in, his receding sockets
glittering from shadows
immobile regards me
out of my own head at me

     who remember:

Then in December in Sixty
his divorced wife my mother
& his sisters & my uncle
& my brothers & my sister
     chat beside my father's velvet
             purple coffin
My tall Uncle Ross presses
his large hairy hand on
my thin shoulder & I
look down at dad & then
his sewn eyes open tearing the torturing threads.

        eyelids
        sealed hinges
        door thousand years secret
        rust & webs of it
        & blood drying in the lashes
        pale blue receding

sockets gazing
out
& the sewn lips too
wrenching at speech, for me

Blown by death out of my spurting into the mouth of death
Carressed to a death passion & sudden
vision of a dead Negro. Outside

in the rustling
night larvae
hang from trees.
Birds sleep.

The moon is pure decaying
all the trees stretch dying on the roads
generation speeds continuous wrecks
windshields spill wind & insects
He lies near sleeping, who
shall be dust in a coffin, whose
eyes shall open up out of me
looking far back to see
every hard body soft & dead.

I press my whole palm to the roof of his head
to sense the deep/sweet
tired tinglings his
own presentiments. I'd
like to know the way he knows I'll die.   Outside

gray larvae
& little eggs
gather
city dust.

FIFTH MESSAGES:
from Samuel Beckett

At evening
with his face to the huge sun

       twilit irises shattering
       the sight too much each
       blink splintering retinae
       gurgling
              volcanic thick
              gorgeous cries
              unstoppered & the sun
              sinks inside:
       wrapped in all that dusk pubic hair
       burnishing. He
stalks dumb/eyes luminous
long hands swinging
lunges into night with
the bright hot sun in his lungs

gasping sunlight all pores
sphincters exploding light in
night his great nude caverns curves
crusty skin & callouses dust/
feet shit thighs emitting what
astonishes binds grafts to/
gether the pale/lusting/hungry
From oxygen of sun in his jut/
ting veins such light shock such
phosphorescent ice white blue as
his hands bone out grab grasp
knead his tongue flickers licks
     secreting heavy glow

       the dogs bark leap & fall
       whine lay their snouts in his ankles
       or rough tongues & fangs hook in in
       shining back chest loins legs
       to hang & dangle like leeches
          for life while
       sunlight drips from their tails

                                        claw dig deep furrows
                                        drink the screams

        that swim
        in his blood
        Sunrays metem/
        psychosis
        waiting
        sounds seeds
        awaiting full bloom of the solar idea
                then to gush
                petals of noise
                urgent black
                fragrant utterance
                not only panic

but of whatever seed it is/ sun embryo
        the brass the drum the stretched
                                fibre/gut
            the tone of the thought

        an ear for sunlight:
        drink the sighs
        or sobs   curses
        claw dig deep furrows
        & drink his prayers

unheard colors of
                    sun.

rhapsody Macaulay not historian his story

what without speech we knew and could not say   what without love we touched
pronouncing good   what without touch we loved and gave no sign   dark
brooding and richly spoken   Macaulay shakes his fist to the heavens   an actor
of creative imagination   nor what he spake   though it lack'd form a little
was not like madness   there's something in his soul   o'er which his melancholy
sits on brood   his grandmother's bones tell secrets   the falcon tethered to his
pulse   his sons tell tales as they wait   But—suddenly—I realized what a poet
is   what you and Charlie and Federico and two or three others are   fountain
would be closer   forever since birth alone hometown hero   used to scream at
his blue apartment walls because he was   I wish I had an excuse to really hate
you   your hands once touched this table and this silver   captures the sweet of
the role with high good humor   the avowed bachelor both in appearance and
disposition   music I heard with you was more than music   all that was once so
beautiful is dead   because of the evel lurking in his own breast   Charles
viewed in the silver   whose days attend his wants   somnambulistic nurses
his sons tell tales as they wait   we need not destroy the past: it is gone   hold to
him in truth and loyalty   this is without blame   truth like a full earthen bowl
thus in the end   good fortune comes from without   everybody knows that in
countries where homosexuality is illegal   you gave me a very important gift
loneliness   you could listen to my Peter Paul and Mary records   I could cook
you lots of roast beef and potato salad   fountain would be closer   whipped at
some length and branded down belly and thighs to show that   his leg cut off as
once before his heart   a proud but covetous moral yet immoral man   mettle
should compose nothing but males   nature seems dead   and wicked dreams
abuse   make use of his fine   deep voice   Macaulay makes an imposing
Macbeth as has been said   it might reappear and seem to be and be the present
would it be a repetition?   only if we thought we owned it   there is not rest of
life   life is one   without beginning   without middle   without ending
Charles   viewed in the silver   whose days attend his wants   somnambulistic
nurses   the old dog inside him lies so still   mourning the death of the family
and the burning down of the house   that is a disease of the mind is solitude   to
be left alone: for this makes an infectious bed   my soule is still in an infectious
body   whipped at some length and branded down belly and thighs to show that
limitations of sadism as a practical way of life are   next time I will hurt him
more   last time I only . . . next time I will . . . even better   everybody knows
that in countries where homosexuality is illegal   which means mainly England
and the United States   the great majority of homosexuals are just like the great
majority   forever since birth alone hometown hero   used to scream at his blue
apartment walls because he was   I wish I had an excuse to really hate you

50

when first they put the name of king upon me   and put a barren scepter in my
gripe   fault   that some have a tendency to strike poses   Macaulay makes an
imposing Macbeth as has been said   we need not destroy the past: it is gone
it might reappear and seem to be and be the present   the concept: the
beginning middle and meaning   from what it considers to be the rest of life
Charles viewed in the silver   somnambulistic nurses   the old dog inside him
lies so still   mourning the death of the family   and the burning down of the
house   in the Grave I may speak through the stones, in the voice of my friends
here I am mine own Ghost   they conceive the worst of me now   whipped at
some length and branded down belly and thighs to show that   limitations of
sadism as a practical way of life are   next time I will hurt him more   last time
I only . . . next time I will . . . even better   that is a disease of the mind   is
solitude   to be left alone   for this makes an infectious bed   my soule is still in
an infectious body   whipped at some length and branded down belly and thighs
to show that   limitations of sadism as a practical way of life are   next time I
will hurt him more   last time I only . . . next time I will . . . even better   if
good   why do I yield to that suggestion   against the use of nature? present
fears   are less than horrible imaginings   he is noble but as he stalks his prey
he is a monster   we feel deeply the heavy burden of guilt he carries   his
destruction has been self-willed   his regret does not leave us   and Verlaine
dead—with all his jades and mauves   and Rimbaud dead in Marseilles with a
vision   his leg out off   as once before his heart   a master of comic timing
bene dick of insolent charm and grace   enjoys every minute of it   Charles,
viewed in the silver   whose days attend his wants   somnambulistic nurses
waiting in the meadow   it furthers one to abide in what endures   no blame
waiting on the sand   there is some gossip   the end brings good fortune
waiting in the mud   brings about the arrival of the enemy   would it be a
repetition? only if we thought we owned it   contemplation of my life   decides
the choice   between advance and retreat   fountain would be closer   forever
since birth alone hometown here   used to scream at his blue apartment walls
because he was   I wish I had an excuse to really hate you   to be left alone: for
this makes an infectious bed   my soule is still in an infectious body   death is at
a young mans backe   and saies nothing   a wretched   private man   dyed of so
poore a Joy as to be declard that hee was a good Poet   mettle should compose
nothing but males   nature seems dead and wicked dreams abuse   he is noble
but as he stalks his prey he is a monster   we feel deeply the heavy burden of
guilt he carries   I don't want to take away your uniqueness   you garlic   you
sapphire you clotted axeltree   what without speech we knew and could not say
what without love we touched pronouncing good   what without touch we loved
and gave no sign   captures the swwet of the role with high good humor   the
avowed bachelor   both in appearance and disposition   trying to hide behind
inadequate shrubbery   it might reappear and seem to be the present   would it

51

be a repetition? only if we thought we owned it   anything may happen and it all
does go together   there is no rest of life   life is one   the more severe it is the
greater the pleasure   sadism is presumably as old as mankind   or older   to a
mysterious place   fucked by four men in succession   the chain which will be
fixed to your collar will keep you more or less flat on your bed for several hours of
the day   in the Grave I may speak through the stone   in the voice of my friends
in the accents of those wordes   which their love may afford my memory   here I
am mine own Ghost   they conceive the worst of me now   death is at a young
mans backe and saies nothing   the dead man spoke to me and begged a penny
I saw his eyes wide open and he stared   through me as if my bones and flesh
were nothing   captures the sweet of the role with high good humor   we will
proceed no further in this business   mettle should compose nothing but males
nature seems dead and wicked; dreams abuse   captures the sweet of the role
with high good humor   the avowed bachelor   both in appearance and
disposition   trying to hide behind inadequate shrubbery   we need not destroy
the past: it is gone   it might reappear and seem to be and be the present
would it be a repetition?   only if we thought we owned it   the concept:
beginning middle and meaning   comes form a sense of self which separates
itself   from what it considers to be the rest of life   by 5a.m. I was all moved in
and feeling better   room 1041   you gave me a very important gift   loneliness
put rancours in the vessel of my peace   tall   manly well-built   what without
speech we knew and could not say   what without love we touched pronouncing
godd   what without touch we loved and gave no sign   a proud but covetous
moral yet immoral man   so strong masculine and plastic   because of the evil
lurking in his own breast   now about material: is it interesting? it is and it isn't
but one thing is   certain if one is making something which is to be nothing the
one making must   love and be patient with the material he chooses   o my
offence is rank   it smells to heaven   try what repentance can   what can it not?
o wretched state   o bosom black as death   turning to the summit for
nourishment   deviating from the path   to seek nourishment from the hill
continuing to do this brings misfortune   turning away from nourishment
perseverance brings good fortune   do not act thus for ten years   nothing
serves to further   turning to the summit   for provision of nourishment
brings good fortune   spying about with sharp eyes   like a tiger with insatiable
craving   no blame   turning away from the path   to remain persevering
brings good fortune   one should not cross the great water   the source of
nourishment   awareness of danger brings good fortune   it furthers one to
cross the great water   everybody knows that in countries where homosexuality
is illegal   which means mainly England and the United States   the great
majority of homosexuals are just like the great majority   still when we return to
that Meditation   that Man is a World   we find new discoveries   and whosoever
hath this Joy   hath a desire to communicate   it   perfits the happiness of Kings

to confer to transfer honor and riches and as they can health upon those
that need   I think I've discovered the world   it itsn't worth a turd   against
the use of nature? present fears   a master of comic timing   bene dick of
insolent charm and grace   enjoys every minutes of it   not going out of the
gate and the courtyard   brings misfortune   penetration under the bed
priests and magicians are used in great number   good fortune   no blame   o
my offence is rank it smells to high heaven   try what repentance can   what
can it not?   o wretched state o bosom black as death   which means mainly
England and the United States   forever since birth alone hometown hero
used to scream at his blue apartment walls because he was   I wish I had an
excuse to really hate you   after I got the money I prepared myself dinner I
have become inordinately fond of chicken livers   you gave me a very important
gift loneliness   you could listen to my Peter Paul and Mary records   I could
cook you lots of roast beef and potato salad   what without love we touched
pronouncing good   a master of comic timing   bene dick of insolent charm
and grace enjoys every minute of it   if good why do I yield to that suggestion
against the used of nature? present fears   are less than horrible imaginings
enjoy every minute of it   the memory be green   and that it us befitted   yet so
far hath discretion fought with nature   how is it that the clouds still hang on
you?   his sons tell tales as they wait   now about material: is it interesting? it
is and it isn't but one this is   certain   if one is making something which is to
be nothing the one making must   love and be patient with the material he
chooses   o my offence is rank it smells to heaven   try what repentance can
what can it not?   o wretched state o bosom black as death   to be left alone:
for this makes an infectious bed   whipped at some length and branded down
belly and thighs to show that   I saw his eyes wide open and he stared   a
proud but covetous moral yet immoral man   we will proceed no further in this
business   mettle should compose nothing but males   nature seems dead and
wicked dreams abuse   tall manly well-built   makes one of the best I have
encountered   magic remains inexhaustible   for like the hectic in my blood he
rages   a kind of wick or snuff that will abate it   for goodness.... dies in his
own too much   but—suddenly—I realized what a poet it   what you and
Charlie and Federico and two or three others are   fountain would be closer   I
am so proud so aloof I kick myself Of course it's my soul I'm talking
about   my temples and sideburns are quite gray now   and Verlaine dead—
with all his jades and mauves   and Rimbaud dead in Marseilles with a vision
his leg cut off as once before his heart   fault that some have a tendency to
strike poses   makes use of his fine deep voice Macaulay makes an imposing
Macbeth as has been said   a kind of wick or snuff that will abate it
everybody knows that in countries where homosexuality is illegal   of course
it's my soul I'm talking about   that it a disease of the mind is solitude   my
soule is still in an infectious body   but I did get drunk and then a little sick

and suddenly like poisonous vomit   what without speech we knew and could
not say   what without touch we loved and gave no sign   fault that some have a
tendency to strike poses   I need to be hugged rather desperately   just now
mettle should compose nothing but males   an actor of creative imagination
was not like madness   there's something in his soul   going leads to obstructions
coming leads to great good fortune   it furthers one to see the great man   how
is it that the clouds still hang on you?   the concept: beginning middle and
meaning   my own walls in which to sink into soft shits of self-pity   whipped at
some length and branded down belly and thighs to show that   that is a disease
of the mind is solitude   to be left alone: for this makes an infectious bed   my
soule is still in an infectious body   whipped at some length and branded down
belly and thighs to show that limitations of sadism as a practical way of life are
next time I will hurt him more   last time I only . . . next time I will . . . even
better   hath borne his faculties so meek   hath been so clear   in his great
office   that his virtues will plead like angels trumpet-tongu'd   against the deep
damnation of this taking-off   a master of comic timing   bene dick of insolent
charm and grace   enjoys every minute of it   Charles   viewed in the silver
whose days attend his wants   somnambulistic nurses   without beginning
without middle   without ending   I am still that incompetent one   that glob of
flailing   after I got the money   I prepared myself dinner   I have become
inordinately fond of chicken livers   by 5 a.m. I was all moved in and feeling
better   room 1041   you could listen to my Peter Paul and Mary records   I
could cook you lots of roast beef and potato salad   well, February seems to be
rushing at me with terrible speed and I am not 20¢ closer to New York   hope
and dream with me   of my precipitate arrival on your shores   still when we
return to that Meditation   that Man is a World   we find new discoveries   and
whosoever hath this Joy   hath a desire to communicate   it perfits the
happinesse of Kings   to confer   to transfer honor and riches and as they can
health   upon   those that need   and Verlaine dead—with all his jades and
mauves   and Rimbaud dead in Marseilles with a vision   tall   manly   well-built
makes one of the best I have encountered   magic remains inexhaustible   what
without speech we knew and could not say   what without love we touched
pronouncing good   what without touch we loved and gave no sign   notable
chiefly because codpieces   do not comprehend intricate fornication   a good
performance by a discovery from television   masculine and hauntingly polite
the melancholy Dane   holds up the skull of Yorick   his grandmother's bones
tell secrets   the falcon tethered to his pulse   his sons tell tales as they wait   it
is as though my heart is absolutely dry and sterile   still when we return to that
Meditation   that Man is a World   we find new discoveries   hath born his
faculties so meek   hath been so clear in his great office   a master of comic
timing   what without speech we knew and could not say   what without love
we touched pronouncing good   what without touch we loved and gave no sign

enjoys every minute of it   now about material: is it interesting? it is and it isn't
but on thing is   certain   if one is making something which is to be nothing   the
one making must   love and be patient with the material he chooses   o
wretched state   o bosom black as death   Charles   viewed in the silver
anything may happen and it all does go together   there is not rest of life   life is
one   without beginning without middle without ending   well-adjusted people
who are perfectly happy beating each other up in private   death is at a young
mans backe   and saies nothing   a wretched private man   dyed of so poore a Joy
as to be declard that hee was a good Poet   as long as we can   let us admit as
much helpe as we can   the more severe it is   the greater is the pleasure   still
when we return to that Meditation   that man is a World we find new discoveries
and whosoever hath this Joy hath a desire to communicate   it perfits the
happiness of Kings   to confer   to transfer   honor and riches and   as they can
health   upon those that need   that his virtues will plead like angels trumpet
tongu'd   out lack of obvious   fabulous success   it could just be our badge of
honor   fault that some have a tendency to strike poses   makes use of his fine
deep voice   Macaulay makes an imposing Macbeth as has been said   and
Verlaine dead—with all his jades and mauves   and Rimbaud dead in Marseilles
with a vision   his leg cut off   as once before his heart   dark brooding and
richly spoken   Macaulay shakes his fist to the heavens   an actor of creative
imagination   masculine and hauntingly polite   the melancholy Dane   holds
up the skull of Yorick   a jug of wine a bowl of rice with it   earthen vessels
simply handed in thought the window   there is certainly no blame in this
bound with cord and ropes   and shut in between thorn-hedged prison walls:
for three years one does not find the way   misfortune   in the Grave I may
speak through the stones   in the voice of my friends   in the accents of those
wordes   which their love may afford my memory   here I am mine own Ghost
they conceive the worst of me now   to a mysterious place   fucked by four men
in succession   to teach you that you are entirely devoted to something outside
yourself   I am still that incompetent one   that glob of wild flailing   as long as
we can   let us admit as much helpe as we can   we will proceed no further in
this business   a good performance by a discovery form television   what
without speech we knew and could not say   what without love we touched
pronouncing good   what without touch we loved and gave no sign   dark
brooding and richly spoken   Macaulay shakes his fist to the heavens
masculine and hauntingly polite   the melancholy Dane   holds up the skull of
Yorick   his grandmother's bonus tell secrets   the falcon tethered to his pulse
how is it that the clouds still hang on you?   there is no rest of life life is one
here I am mine own Ghost   they conceive the worst of me now   and whosoever
hath this Joy   hath a desire to communicate   in the Grave I may speak through
the stones   in the voice of my friends   in the accents of those wordes   which
their love may afford my memory   here I am mine own Ghost   they conceive

the worst of me now   still when we return to that Meditation   that Man is a
World we find new discoveries   and whosoever hath this Joy   hath a desire to
communicate   it perfits the happiness of Kings to confer   to transfer   honor
and riches   and   as they can   health   upon those that need

(Structure: chance operations after arbitrary choices; Method: coin method
based on the I Ching; structural elements: I Ching; Discordants, Preludes of
Memnon (XLV) (LVIII), Time in the Rock (XLVI) by Conrad Aiken; Macbeth;
Reviews of Macbeth and Much Ado About Nothing; Hamlet; Charles, viewed
in the silver; Lecture on Nothing, by John Cage; Eros Denied by Wayland
Young; Devotions Upon Emergent Occasions by John Donne; Letters, Hickman
to Macaulay, 2/16/64 and 4/4/64; Letters, Macaulay to Hickman, 1/10/64,
1/13/64, 2/21/64 and 3/17/64.)

EARLY TIRESIAS

Tiresias I:I

RAIN RAIN TIRESIAS BLIND WORD-RAIN
inside   clouds black wrap me rain
Tiresias   witchman shapeshifter shaman
        slurp up
wordpour   scare up your lifesong   out
from your god-dead birdgut vision Tiresian,   blow-
job-grum Tiresian word-rain/ up, rise
up/ your snakesplitting stick erect
high over memory snakebed: Blue
        peppertree   flies   haze
shimmer down secrets   I want to
see what you look like   under your
levis   under your shorts   I want to
see have you got hairs where I have   let's
climb this peppertree naked together
shout out cries of sunburnt weeds
sprint with hard-ons over the bluffs
speed on bicycles   no hands
& give the finger to skies with both
hands as we go   Youth-green
eyes   & all that   time & again I
I come from the ground on change-scent
never enough for me never enough
see me lap it up it is blood it
        is to be living again, a little a-
            live, no
        matter how, no matter how
brief   life   life again   Fuck me
I've come to your bare room it glows now
twilight outside   weed-heavy rain
no sound of the city   I've come to
revive you at cycle-hush   Come
        to say to you look outside
the hospital yard on bloomfire
you're not going to die grandma you're just
not   Your hands slide over me   hot
summer rain in them

What are you whispering I
do not hear   not too near to
you   You never expected cunt to
to pulse with the pulse of rainfall
         What are you
whispering grandma   oh dying's not—
Pulse, flux & mindsurge   dweller in
earthlight
     rain thru the window
          I've come to
burst the deathskin off you   fuck
           me.

[1966]

Tiresias I:2

NOW, TIRESIAS
see that far back   chug
of an old black car packed full of women
gasoline leak into earth   stops
beside cleared ground   where tough
men with my young father   heft
the rainsoaked rafters into place
              the women urge
them on: build it squat   tarstained   ugly
like us forever unfinished   death's
shack   I see that far back   Soldier over-
head bunkboy   your sex rage   as this
barracks' gunmen sleep   shakes
our snores off   it's night go to it   fist
wrapped hard tight solo   go go to
your sky in your lonely sheet   toward
the dancer under your lids   jack let
your noises wake them   so each bunk
trembles   each hand grasps each his
good cock   speechless in
a rain of rustling under company moon &
hear nightlong storm of gasps you've started
quick privates quivering in their dreams single
handed raising the creaking roof &
listen to the progress of the shudder   bunk
9 bunk 5 bunk 21 & 12   everyone comes
then dawn comes   be lulled by lapping of
whitecapped hisses between white teeth   I
see again muscles building it windy
cursing each other's work
& the hard warped timbers:
Tiresias, grow here (& there will be
hunters under my house   snakes &
black widows)   I'm high so I'll tell you
I remember my ancestor fullblooded Cherokee
his breath in my ears as he holds me
Go down I love you I love you go down
by sea under stars it
is summer   go down on us   I see

his black eyes   lined face
                        as he holds me, a baby
as he whispers soft to me   wild   I'm high so
I'm telling you   Our feet in cool waves
our bodies in sand   Later they told me
he'd been dead for a century   Spanish
music over the harbor, the town's
neons shine on the water   go down   go
down   Isn't he part of me
ghost, breathing my breathing   I hold to him
holding me   safe   safe   &
I've never told anyone   Now see
that far back   memory that begins me
old black car chugging uphill   where
angry men hammer where men hammer.

[1966]

Tiresias I:3

AT THE BASE OF MY SPINE NOT DROWNING
floating   his boneless arms   snakes
in the water   his pleading lips
mumbling silences   I peer
down the spine tunnel   I turn him
with my stick   I learn loathing.
she lies on her back   the air-cooler hums
her hair is wet on her forehead
she presses my hand to her belly
he flails with boneless gestures
swells her with words without marrow
I lock the spine's tunnel   close down
eyesight   but he kicks within us
alive thru all changes   My
wife   my sons   to protect them
pistol beneath my pillow   I sleep
with his death to protect them   screw
your sick world over your eyes   brother   you
say you see us   you   don't see us   your
eyes   seek   your eyes   This is the shack
my father built   these are my brothers
this is my mother born without hands
this is the axe my father chose   those
were our hands   Canal by the railway
it swims thru me   child swimmers gone
dusk is in the water   she's gone   she's
gone forever yes   close the door   I
want to sleep   yes here's money   Warm
waters slipping past deep mud as
soft as powders   tall velvet cattails
screen my body from trains   swim up-
stream   strip out of my suit   it
sinks behind me   my skin the
water   bends my stiff cock backward the current
tugs at my balls   None of
you boys have loved me   I don't
know how but I've failed you   Polluted
canal   I am your current I am your cattails

erect along the rails   I cling I sink in-
to you   Somewhere along the line I
I don't know where   I went so wrong   tell
me   help me   On my back   floating
slowly falling   the polluted waters
flow over my face   touch silt & sink
in it   sink in it   You won't answer me
will you so get out get out   Surge over
my own chest & thru my lungs   His arms
underwater   writhe toward me   lock
the spine's tunnel   close down
vision   he does not drown.

[1966]

Tiresias I:4

LIKE A MAN HE SMASHES SOMEONE'S MOTORCYCLE
against a curb   like a man   screams
lands on his ass   back-broken   paralyzed
makes his little pool of piss like a man
white cast chest chafing   naked crotch   like a
man he whines for soup   overalled
he plants the plum   you dropped thru her front
not her gruntybig hole   like a man
bangs the hammer on his thumb   like a man
tries to enlist   4
F   & crashes the car against truck's
side   he brings mother home
she's bleeding in her face & fainting   Watch,
Tiresias   that young man's ass rising & falling
firm white flanks rippling   over that young
ass lifting upward toward that
young man's prick plunging slowly in & out
out & in slowly   that dark head sucking
that yellow head's ears & neck   those
shoulders crushing that prone young
man whose thick legs spread wide are
tan against the sheets   those pale flexed legs
of the fucker as he just tips just edges
in then slides fast down   that gut click   hear
it   that yellow head's exhalation   that
resistless moan   Watch   we're
alone in your room & I undress for you
jacket tie shirt shoes socks & undo
my belt   Okay kid   look: this
window's a mirror   there's the guy   he
can't see you're looking   now you
make him confess   I take off my trousers   look
at my body   no, you can never touch me   So
when we take you to him don't say nothing
okay kid say hi   but what we want to see is
what the freak   does when he sees you   Your
eyes strain to touch me   freak how you
reach for the real   Don't be afraid

point thru the mirror's back   behind
the back of tenderness   at
the slumped back of the accused   In
some icecold moment you'll cry out   you'll
try to touch me   Confront him kid, show him
you're the one who fingered him   Your cry
your fingers   fall thru me   my beauty
is all silence & nothing   Whose love
spat back clamps iron bars around him
These hairs on my body bristle in my sweat
tho I don't move   & you don't touch.

[1966]

Tiresias I:5

HERE EVERYTHING SNAPS IN TWO, TIRESIAS:
    broken woman   red lips & brown
eyes of chaos   auburn hair of chaos
    broken woman   breaking
my eyes   breaking hot glare   stab
of sunlight on stone where you lead me:
   breaks off in your name   in
   unborn consonants of your name
splinters of salt piercing our eyes
glitter & glitter into the brain's
       smallest hardest seed   Gravel
path sunset I kiss the girl   but
beyond her bra-strap catch your gaze
    you'll
get dust on your housedress   pressed
    to the shut screen door
or moths in your auburn hair   not a
flicker of eyelash   not one tic
of your right nostril   not even
an uneven breath   not a word   yes: some
tears that are meant to disturb us   we
tremble   so what   the bird abandonment
flaps against my face   but see
I jerk my head   frightening it
back into auburn shadows of
     orange grove & smudgepots
       & dead sunsets   Abandonment
pecks at my skin   its droppings blur
my freshman peace poem   downstairs
does some secret brilliant boy
ease his $2\frac{1}{2}''$-wide veincluster
deep thru her teenage smile?   Command
that tiny Pfc snap to!   when
was the last time you had a haircut
soldier?   Lucky the tortoise-shell cat
purrs on my bird-splattered page   down-
stairs do tongues meet?   & does he lick
his streaks of gyzm from her teeth?   Dis-

missed!   I tuck my chest-hairs in I
halt him order him softly come back   come
back   salute me blue-eyed private   sa-
lute me   salute us   salute   I stare
at his shineless boots & feel
      shifting of half-light
over the neat white bricks   Front door
squeals   hot rod laughs   she kisses
         me now   as the smells
of his bones & his armpits whip me
bound & gagged with her hair   Squeeze your
chaos into my open mouth   morning glory
tendrils twist your words of salt that
milklike drop on the tongue   the salt
that falls from your mothering lips
blooms thru all pores & fingertips
the hate under our nails   is also you
is you, Tiresias, broken   broken
      woman of   breaking.

                              [1966]

Tiresias I:6

AND I GLIDE, AGAIN ON THE OLD MEAT LOOKOUT
        my beak splitting the hail of
ashes in ashlight   soaring
on the reeking wind above the parched bluffs
high over heavyheaped melted tracks the
crusted blisters of canal mud the rows of
charred electric poles the splintered
homes   the bent & windowless cars
      rusting in crumbling streets   my
shadow invisible over the black front lawns
as I screech my name in the silence   Kid
   drones   but I in slacks & sunflow
   resting my wise ass on the backsteps
brushing my mancut grey hair   pain of my
girl chick's night teeth yet stopping up
   pores of my fat breasts   scratched
   by my sweatshirt   am   really am
the real live quiet queen bee   slurping &
splashing her lips in her honey but he   he
   still seeks & buzzes   his
floppy sweet stinger hangs limp in my skin
   And I spy you dead little boy
   fallen in the tattered outskirts
in your indian leggings   your cubscout-rite-
lipsticked thin bare chest   your
nipples circled   your navel swastika'd
   a meat-red halfmoon scribbled
over your eyelids   withered under war-
feathers   flat on your back   near
   the shriveled garden-hose the
   chalkwhite mounds of dog turds
waiting   Or for hours on end we play ping-
   pong mother or
watch the guys making out Her toreador
   pants slither down   she
nibbles my thumb   With that black girl
in the sunshine on benches   & the trusties
   winking & smiling or   Rain comes
in thru my window   leaps from my

prick to her tongue   Else we pick beans some-
times the guys whisper don't you dare squeal
on us faggot when   Bobby is
    ashes   & Billy is ashes   the
house
    is empty   I dug for Tiny
but no dog's there   & the turtle
    burned up in David's hand &
David & Jerry   their hair on fire
& big black wings cut my face   claws
    cut my chest   We try to escape   or
I pray 1000 hail marys to save me
from the criminal insane hospital &
Raindrops splash on her ankles her knees rain-
    drops on the nape of my neck rain
    rain drenching my hair   I
had a rather long mind test too dad
dad do they have any answers?
    The beak lets the wind thru my eyes the
        beak lets the wind have my throat.

[1966]

70

Tiresias I:7

      BLACK JALOPY
backfiring in swelter   insects
      throb like rain on the pitted windshield
   the old man spits thru the window   we
   bump over a
   snake in the road   do you
   see it mashed flat in the road?
we enter steep mountains, the shadows   truck
stop!   no dr peppers! no damn dr peppers! the wind
     clangs low in the
     jaw
        always the mountains Tiresias crosses, this
        not the only dark range dark summit to
        conquer, this
        not the only Old Ridge Road uncoiling   Crease
of Lt Cartwright's green fatigues could slice
   flesh   Winding toward the cold cold summit
His huge thumbs hooked in his web-belt clamped to his
   you can't call it gut
steel navel   alright, Fuckup
   haircut   haircut   haircut as his
metal tongue dances down the middle of my back
& the orderly room shimmies in sweat blur while
while sunlight splatters the white bricks golden
   How could it be a dream?   I remember
he crooned to me as he held me   he isn't dead
he's here   now   with us
                Mountain lions
asleep in fields of blue lupines, rattlesnakes
asleep on boulders, tarantulas in the sand of
picnic stops, hoboes by drinking fountains
carved in the cliff-face, accidents,
bodies bleeding in the road's soft shoulder   upward
   Little baby sister with mysterious eyes   this is for you
     reach out   touch it thru the bars of your crib
     here, it is new, do you like it?   it's yours
my erector set my chemistry set my terrier my dreams
      my erector set my chemistry set my terrier my
      dreams   Silver sea beyond sudden valleys   Let me

caress your pink lips with it
      your little fist cannot open yet
        don't let it go   Downward
now my old jalopy rattles downward   Mom says
    quick look there's the ocean Cliff says
where Johnny says I like the ocean I like the
     Dad whistles chiri-biri-bin
     Grandpa spits thru the window   the dogs
bark scamper scattering potato chips we enter
new homeland the mountains level   have we left the mountains?
     for all the meadows grow yellow & green   look
there's the ocean   there are poppies   scarlet white
orange downward to orchards orchards   look! look!
      have we, have we left the mountains?
       Salute he says & afterward
            twilight
       engulfs us both in privacies
           his gaze
       shifts to my boots I await his command
               willingly
    Have we, have we left the mountains?
    When they told me he was dead, told me
I had never seen him, when they said it was a dream
& that dreams are unreal, are lies, I opened the car door
as we sped along & was snapped out into the wind.
they grabbed me. did I hold on. nevertheless
I'm dead, don't you see, now that there is nothing
strong anymore
    On the sea's edge   foamspray in slow motion
    tips the grey wing   flashes turquoise & emerald
     we plunge into the thrashing mountain

                               [1967]

Tiresias I:8:A

THAT THIS COW SHOULD DIE & THE HEIFER TOO
     is not permitted
    these rabbits scrunched in hutches
    pooping pellets thru wire floors
    pissing forever, tireless pissing
these chickens clucking in stinking
turds this spotted dog shitting in alfalfa
these lazy eucalyptus
   trees, bitter in the fat breeze, these
   ducks, these tomatoes, these aphids in the roses
o christ these small potatoes
  Tiresias hide us in the light hide us in the light hide us
  And I'm laughing laughing confronted
  by the handcuffed child whose fear
  betrays me the cock he drinks from some
  sweaty times in a concrete tearoom by the sea they're
  taking me away quiet quite far my wife kids
  freeze in the door so trapped in a calm the
  boy is so young the dicks so straight the crime so
  so much ecstasy to crow for I pet my
    car green clean polished in the sun
            O my hair
   floats over the hard-on the grown-up's
   get stuck in my throat I dig
    them out my knees
   slide on canal silt, I suck I tongue
    down up, underwater, a
    boy's job & come
     up for air near his nipples,
    wave to the Daylight Limited (the canal
    does muffle boxcars) he breast strokes bare-
    assed under the road-bridge white
    frog thru the cattails far out
     of sight I count
    boxcars Tiresias will hide us in the light
And saltcome drips from roofbeam, leaf
point feather point as the red cock
preens & pecks in the barn rabbit pelts
glisten in the rafters horseflies suck & fuck

dead lizards & lemons burst open
chickenhawks soar above cowdung
dirtclods swarm with monarchs, white
moths   smudgepot milkweed sea-
salt & skunk spurt fugues in the air
    caterpillars writhe in the anise, while
the sun shoots bullseye after bullseye over
the mother mounds down to the dripping farm   What
    I'm so hot to be I'm blinded by   the Lean
    Corporal stripped-down struts thru the barracks
        I spy him among the cadre cursing the coffee or
        sullen   sizing up our tender asses
        snarled at chewed out   heartsmitten in close
        ranks I nervily glance into his govt issue gaze &
        his govt issue frown cuts thru the sunlight at me
            lights out in my bunk my fingers sprout his Italian
            hairs they track over my skin like shivering
moonprobes   from falling in to falling out & in the hard-hit
sack his unclaimed buddy apes his spitting smoking kiss-
my-shaggy-ass repose   & takes it like him, learns from
        him to take it   My farm,
        I will not move you from where you are
        I'll let you be   your only home is here
        roses, & bees that really sting, I will not
        move you from where you are   flying
        ants, mining the beanfield ranges, who
        notices your signaling wings?   but I
        will let you be your home is here   Lone
sleeper in empty barracks, wakes: the Lean
Corporal bends over my bunk   staring
                            into my dream
      (why were you watching me sleeping?)   no
                        answer
        no one stirs   (how long have you stood here
        watching me sleeping?)   no
        answer   I nearly whisper (you've been
        ordered to wake me every day?)   no
answer   in darkness he moves to the stairhead,
halts   his leather voice whips thru the hollow
bldg: be awake when I come around, cocksucker
    makes me sick what you look like a-
        sleep/ I might

       puke on you   No,
you don't have the guts to murder   in
this prison burn out pity & fear   no
time for that chore once you're free, once
you've hunted him down   Canal,
    I am your current I am your cattails, sky-
    clad   floating on my back, toward
    the low underpass, the spine-tunnel
    where wet bugs & frogs feed on the wet dark Cornsilk
tassels beanstalk tendrils have their home here
they can't die   roses bees flying ants their
breath the smoke out of lemon groves curling
above the big yawn of fields
beans & hay where cow & heifer nuzzling never
diseased bloat up   they can't
    die/ if ripped from the sun, the farm's
      blood   Tiresias spills
    from pasture woodlot barn & coop until it
      crumples   chickens rabbits
          torn to shreds
        bleeding mouth & beak, then I/
        but it can't/ no. no. no. no./ it
        can't die.

                    [1968]

Tiresias I:8:B

LIKE AN OLD WOMAN, THIN WHITE HAIR STILL
    strung on her scalp,
                  whimpering I
    don't wanna die I don't wanna die (my
    ear on her sour lips to hear) my
    farm dies o dragonfly skeleton
brittle legs crush brittle stem the blunt
pipe iron thuds behind the softpink soft twitch-
in ears cracking small brain & flooding
    gush thru nostrils no my blood-
drenched dad kills each rabbit one by
one no no each creaturely alarmshriek—
    cows   pierced against barbs   bellowing
    ants   scatter   scatterover furrows
    birds   flutteringstunned   huddled in
corners/ all,beasts,cornered,die,screeching,NO
    cornshocks stormdumb &
    deaf to the   sound-
track/ Tiresias   Imprisoned in screams of I
    will kill him hunt him kill him kiss him suck him
    off little boy kill him who hides me in the light.
how should I know what prison's done to Bob it's crap—
fantasy   grey hair cropped short   a shot of him
handing in his locked razor   close-up: bent, in-
tent upon prisonfarm workshop machinery   jump
cut: nightmare of his nightmare his hunky prick
gouging,spurting,choking my throat as I dreamdie, you
    see, in his dream I'm still a kid   in mine he
    stabs me in the back on a treelined street &
stabs my wife when she comes down the steps behind me
    Young tykes swam here there was much horse-
    play such groping too & grade A goosebumped
asses fresh peachfuzz sprouting, spanking clean &
        lifted wet from the canal for train
        passengers, defenseless sightseers   I
would sneak my fingers beneath the waterline
lingering in cattails while naked acquaintances
stroked from bank to bank thru the stiff current.

Like I study his teeth while he sleeps my nuts
        full of jizz that yellow
how I'd like to make him drink my—but
                                my CO's waiting some-
times I settle my boot on his ribs so soft he
        keeps on snoring his eye-
lids sweat I blow in his ears I spy his
        boner sneak under his sheet just a sneak in a sheet but
                        my CO's waiting some-
times I hold my head right down close to his
        lips   dangle
spitstreams he swallows like queers in their dreams. my
CO's waiting   Now by the deserted canal
            despondent in pussywillows   flared
                    nostrils in the stench of
        sludge/scum bulging under the under-
        pass   slacks tho no train's running slipped
        to my ankles   bleak sky overhead a-
          las smoke up from factory
        stacks, pounding my pud amid high parched reeds as
        nearby on turquoise emerald slick float dead
        pollywogs   gray bellies burst at dusk alas.
Follow inner skulltrack pan probe motion out-
        ward blink flesh shudders wide &
light meets deep brown hate-eyes' stare in halfdark
        spittle out of his halfsmile slow-
        motion drips sparkling   quick the
bedsheet blocks frame, bottom to top   flash-
back-cut to dreaming soldier probe wet pale
dawnskin hangjaw thin ribs rising, falling, sheet
down, tangled on hairy young loins & look look the
enemy hard-on eye peeks out   glistens to shoot
    you drip your panic on yellowteeth   sound-
track blurts fastbackpan rapid dolly downstairs past
latrinemirror glanceshot re loneliness/snarl & tracks
out in company street where Tiresias with his staff
    blindsockets shoots your unedited life   Man
steps from bus which moves out of our story   he
    walks & you're close at his back   off-
camera voice bruises his name he aboutfaces shock the
arm the knife slash into the frame & he falls bleeding

cells of his face screeching/
run murderer run run your vision raging, holding your
        free action jerking in your own hands once
    twice   panning back to view me   lying where
            ever you'll leave me, whatever sidewalk, what-
            ever slick streetset   under harshlight
                in rain.   liquid-
dissolve   O bad movies o bad movies
birds yellowteetch stiff current mouth & beak
I study his teeth whatever sidewalk pussywillows ants
boner sneak what prison's done your only home is
here hairy young loins his hunky prick pollywogs
stripped-down struts screeching cells stroked
flooding gush shaggy ass repose prisonfarm work-
    shop parched reeds signaling track over my
skin bruises his name naked writhe in the anise
                Tiresias
        enemy hard-on dreamdie boxcars red cock
bedsheet blocks frame free action jerking   cow
        & heifer hard-hit sack burn out pity &
fear white frog rabbit pelts wet pale dawn-
skin burst at dusk torn to shreds stabs me in the
    back sludge/scum mother mounds/our
tender asses vision raging underpass alarmshriek
flesh shutters dicks so straight stuck in my throat horseflies
o bad movies   haphazard editor of
        movies   o very heavy movies.

                        [1969]

TIRESIAS I:9:A

AND THESE MY PECKERS   LICK THE LOVELIES
George 40   Bob 33   Conway 17   Larry 28, their weekly
     childsplay, age 12, public library rest-
     room California coast town   down on
     big kneebones sliding their hairy
     grownup crotches forward over red
tilefloor until each omotherallmine is mine, with
               lips in a frenzy I peek
over navels under marble
               booth di-
vider to see their fatherly masks fall
     off as something crazy happens, can't
     reckon what   tho my raw tongue tastes
     it, relishes saltgoo   hot   sweet   swift
     budding upon buds   input/output
center for wet music carressucking, al-
most wriggling I burrow my heart in their groins, in-
most peter rabbit still/ their utmost special
     thrill of the week   fastrising child-
star halfbuck I remember them by sizes halfbuck & how
much hair how slow or quick their grins come
     (these my peckers, when I lick lovely).
Yes Lee this is before your dad goes bald or begins
looking old   before he's killed   he dreams
adrift thru dawn-light groaning.
36, but this day age-wrenched, an angry
vastation under foglit
                    sheets   when
he wakes. you're here in a doorway, boy,
watching.
          pillows on blue linoleum, your mother
nowhere at all in the house   torn
linenclutch round him like rope
& where could she go, &
what can be done without
lunchmoney?   wakes. coughs. fumbles a
Lucky. you
          light it. please dad can I have some
lunchmoney?   writhes   hacking   throat-

                    gears stripping   iceblues
                    clenched shut, smoke-
                    smarting   frown & bark: your
                    mother's gone dammit she's left us for
                    good. gone? forever? yes Sonny
gone   Wet
window bursts from dreaming skull, night-
flash (Ginny asleep beside me, her
            black dog whimpers beneath our bed)
revealing thru dark the far-off
blazing of the nimbus'd god, golden, naked, his
stern gaze searing
            not thru my eyes but thru this
wrenching of my forehead (skin & bone, clean-
            severed by nightblast)
            & descending   strong   upon me:
stop here.   stop.   words
will shrivel up, burn
singed at the songheart,
      flux will lose lightning—

As fresh & as   clean as a smooth
bean just pod   poppt jesus he's skin &
bones hairless my   son no older/ by
tapping one's toes on a   johnfloor! what's the
use? crashing down male   storm deafening
glandular thunder it's   lighting-lad his
flick rip at my zip. thirst. thirst. christ first make
breath calm set down   briefcase, prop
wide his frostglass door don't be afraid. Lois! Lois!
& what of his homelife? ask him innocent ghost
pale & do you get   very good grades in school I bet?
For George: bike racked   amid honeysuckle cords
dipped to sneakers &   toilet seat glued to
boybutt eyes   to Shakespeare ears
to footsteps down the basement stairs or else
tensed toward any   neighborbooth & hope
for his cautious   shoetap irongray
head under the wall his   baby blues to peer up begging
fly slack & tie   tucked his shuffle out-
side my door brief-   case & all until
I gape wide: for   for George kid lips

must stretch taut his
rough rhythm lunging I
able to choose between
A's pubes of his testes
bridge sweats as

grasp on ducktail the
gasp against un-
breath & it straight
tickle netherlip nose
sight dims belt

     buckle clinking on hornrims.
Slows   pulls up alongside you   offers
a lift his halo in matchflare o lifts
you   hickman what's happening   are you
mated by miracle his mortal pick-
up will he leave you wildpetaled,
stamened & pistil'd   out
    of this blowing dust?
1961 streetlights passed under make
    gleam the flushed prepuce
  an earlobe brushed against steering wheel
    at times his young knuckles
  an earlobe brushed against tieclasp   burnt
  ripples. until key is turned & motor
dies & that stop-action ascent into slow fade again
in that grainy room   at that dim stairtop
    as nightsmog sighs against neon.

And Angie said, meet Mary Ellen Eleanor Hen
derson & you say
    please call me
Eleanor   I don't let on, I feel a prairie
tremble summery inside of me   but ad-
jacent to that shock juts, plain as a

    silo of loneliness, that
      creaking hollow half-burned-down
barn where dad's leather strap struck
    once too hard, back
    in Nebraska
standing on my head on the beach I feel an
ocean inside me like a moaning woman
watching & praising you watch & praise me.
Mary Ellen Eleanor up in the mother ward

cries with the first one, while dad

This sun-vision, this feverish
    rape, plowing my words in—O
once but once brainfuckt by Apollo!
    once dream-gored, grippt by his gold
thighs, all energy in the cosmos, all heat, all
gentleness (& the wrenchings, the
        wrenchings)
    what can anyone else ever tell you
    what can you do but lie helpless
      beside your girlfriend Ginny
    with her black poodle Ethel under the
bed, whining from ticks, the house-
spider filaments floating in dawn the white
  cat Freddie purring between you? when
I woke I'd soaked the bedding thru with
    sweat, mind full crammed with
        fire, vagina
    of my skull still tender & smoking.

hollers at my braindoor a son of a
    bitch I could hit him & run, it
hangs on us he hangs on us, so you try
more & I whisper more Eleanor Eleanor, back
    in the thirties

better not tell about-it transport
    twisted easily
killed—delirium a disease to get well from—
no/no/I don't want to be cured of you Apollo
    blue sun breath door god!

I like it best
in the concrete
sucks me kisses me
tree or kneeling
or I lean against
dirty old palm
testicles I
face what a hot wild
shrimp has shit I
gnawed in his mouth
his wriggledy ear
prowl past the bushes
& turns me his
squeeze him hard
him kneel down oh
beneath his smooth lips
slapping his eye-
of all I need
by seaside
I smoke he slurps
breathes in our ear
last nothing but truth/ Bob
I love you Bob
& big Bob whisks me
grampclutches to
hidden in oak
settia strips
stand I kneel &
muscles locked mountains
agrowl w/ info Bob's
spittle agleam in head-
fleshbursts chests
sparks scorch
delibly kiss bite
scrounge

he sucks me off
head by seaside
beneath banana
by ivy by oleander
sharp mean hairs of
tree he licks my
squat on his
tongue his young
love my fingers
love my tongue in
while the cops
doltheads
other soft ear I
by his nipples make
like my pink nipples
like my nuts
lids but best
the concrete head
cool salt dark when
& old surf he
the truth at

sweetkidcries/ Dusk
from withered urinal
Alameda Park where
clump soft-skinned poin-
make me naked under the band-
he teaches me ashtaste
bloodprickle caves
prick Lee's
lights bright
shooting off hair
the ladskin brain in-
suck swallow
burn to learn

82

kneel down worship adore.
  Nightsmog smeared against neon
cheap dog furnished room top rear rickety
hollywood down house by parkinglot solitary hot
    plate closet w/Sam
Beckett Bill Faulkner to dusty peeling
    wall tacked/ hickman
here, where you bring grum beauty, in
cufflinks & tieclip & blond frown shine   switch
off the lamp   hide   your makeshift   kick
    dirty socks under the cot, you
reach out to touch him in the dark of
Selma Ave headlights hushing over the ceiling he
puts you off turns aloof in the dark turns
    cold (meaning:
beauty can't touch you not here not ever).

My inland sisters distrust you   I lose
    my jobs   but the war
effort feeds us   so we make more
war   & babies, sticking it out while they grow
    Roosevelt
dies   Lee I have these darn
    headaches headaches 'borderline
amnesia I mean anemia' Lee will this house ever
be finished yes I'm crying the kids fight so darn
    much Lee don't treat them so
mean I hit them for you dammit to shut them
    up Lee the doctor said 'move
    move to a real cool climate.'
christ why can't I be the shore I take us to
    wondering: Eleanor Eleanor
is this where you and dad can't break me, back
    where we met?

Apollo of enlightenment   break
    me out of this mind where
Ginny sleeps where Ethel & Freddie
sleep & unswept cobwebs sway in sea-
    currents near ceiling my
mental body at mid-light your ancient
heat breeding my brain you are born from
    Apollo wherefrom
words sprout where words were not
Apollo who come in a mind like a desert
& here plant messages from the vaster
    far emptier heart-space   spermpollen
    stark against dream drought
Apollo   wound this head real
fierce lord of inwardness thrusting
meatbeam sunrays thru skullcunt, mend
    all my mirrors   break

    me free.   Beauty won't touch you, my
    voice in your mind age 26 thru the scene
    you will always urge out of   in ten years
        to write about   only old truth asighing
    listless, unnoticed   wanding my useless
        snakesplitting stick

as headlights of everypassing autos hush
          over the two of you playing at nightmare the defeat of
   love by hunger by sadness
listen listen won't you hear me
   listen the death in you swimming
  with arms like snakes writhing inside you
hatched out of self-loathing, look what lusts
to snag you to drowning, do you love drowning?

Orgasm's my hobby how
come you never come the grape-
vine's got your number I'm
happy to meet you why
can't you pop don't
you bead off yeah well
right now I weigh a lot but
you oughta see me after
football season
jesus please keep it secret
pop's high school prin-
cipal you're in a
class with my sister?
don't ever tell my
sister well we can try
the library the park the
choirloft in that e-
piscopalian church how
'bout the stairway by
the elevator-shaft in
the county courthouse tower no
one uses it drop your
damn pants drop 'em let
me c'mon turn around bend
over you can take it it's
not so big I'd
love to get you off you
frustrate me well it's like
it's like forget it some
day you'll oh yeah let's
meet right after school's
out/ why? why? be-
cause it feels so, so, oh

Conway I want to be per-
fect you stand out-
side my frostglass
door you show yourself
off   run when I
open   I want to be perfect
then we are brave
enough to hug hello we
are so near in
fears bravery is neces-
sary/ if you can be
brave at 17 I can be
brave at 12
so we climb
the county courthouse tower
elevator-shaft-stair-
way where I let you
give me to your-
self I want to come sky
high too I want to be perfect
I touch your
jacket your belt your fly your
jock I just want to be
perfect it's a feeling of
defeat, of
never being
all to you I'm
scared to
death of
coming Conway
Conway you don't
think I
screw my

84

kid you don't think I screw   face up
my face up grit   hold my breath &
my teeth & groan this way   cry this way

on account of it hurts me do you?
Befuddled body of childhood snagged this
     far into the lonely—
perfected physique of time at hand & bared
     with cool & cruel refusal
to schoolboys by brainslides on burning roads
straining to touch with your gaze
what his bronze hands fondle   hard gold
     fist on gold hard
rod & rough hand thrusting aside
your awkward soft & tentative vain
     reaches for real.
at last you lie back.   & you're nothing &.
     he is all silence & nothing.
    & nothing & nothing &.

Somewhere along the line Eleanor I
I went so wrong   tell me   help
    me   your son's
    asking where are you he's a
boy underwater looking to drown me, none
of my sons have loved me & I raise
my arm with the belt the money, close
the door, I want to sleep   she's
gone she's gone forever yes   Eleanor
Eleanor you won't answer me will you so get
    out get out   & the strap slashes
salt splinters burn here at the back
    of my brain.

Blue sun breath door blind word-rain
    forsake any search any meaning, let
    the search seek you. create
    the alone with no second, defeat
    that sullen other
    coiled coldcockt within you
    unto death. unto death
    to feel my rays on skin you're naked in,
    waking to singing so
    long as you grow
furrowed by burst-time, seeded
by my fresh spermbeams splashing deep
hot into brainsoil dreambeat fertile.

Mexican Larry meets me   he's got a hairy
body his head pokes under the wall I
    poke his meek lips
    all the way in
now mother what's happening my bony
white legs shudder under blue marble wall I'm
agony-squeezed thru stone striations my knees
strapped in flames to the red tilefloor, this

message wall's a quaking wall, this
red tilefloor sears up thru my song it's
shrieking it's shrieking   over & over I'm
wingprickt aloft over bright harsh foothills on bloom-
fire

[1969]

TIRESIAS 1:9:B: GREAT SLAVE LAKE SUITE

Hay River. September 1973

      Husht
squalid like my dad in a grave in my brain, burial of
         verve, blind dumb deaf wet grovel dis-
tances clampt gag & my mindfold tight on me can't
breathe or die Hank & I all my scraggled song dumpt go
         batterd out of night toward Great Slave
Lake this bus rattles over gravel ruts flat long dirt
forest road north one dark & a thin dark day under far-
         off lightning & gray nervous
boreal rainfall my writhen corpse who is me before me
         moans o for me o for me o to destroy me

& once my son dying

o   law I die
under nothing to do with free
kind my brutish
law, out
law miracle, crawl, sweat, to glory, got
adventure & got ascared, dad, dad, my dad a
version, blue eyes under silt by sea not light not light not
work on what has been spoild nor furthers
my work on what has been spoild   o

o   all the poets are Hidden. stoned
occlusion bursts into word-rain, dad songs
me high thru my blue sun breath door I cry I
cry war war my jews my japs die, dad at canal red shoulder white
thigh, hate
him, tell, tell, re-tell, how the time's
hard, oat slabs
float in the lard, dad, grit in the kids' swiss
chard, stink bugs
fart in the yard   o

this song or segment of song for that flawd song Leland at
         26 in 61 tongue out dripping for
         balm in the corrupt
land bereft angry hungry weeping

male snake of that time in my dark those pale hard headlights wove
        over my dusty ceiling from
cars beneath my window, wide open on selma my
        gay young hustlers
lust bereft angry hungry weeping where
Beckett Faulkner at a loss glare down that my
        strong song's urge
        hoist me higher in my malign
fire this song or fragment of song for that snarld song Leland at
        26 in 61 isolate rubble down gutters shuffler in
our thick spit pool of absolute freedoms against the law to be
        legal, heritage bilge trash, out still for
balm in glutton land policemen to kneel to to pray to, mostly a
        lone in Los Angeles aching
all down selma vine to highland hardon bared icy in drizzle shouting
        four a.m. hank cinq at lung top get a guy
fuck me in azaleas spit on my face slap me by the church at las palmas
        way we slay the blue temple/ weird
wanderings of my subtle body

slow motion explosion lone grebe on the beach.
please don't kill me sir please don't kill me sir.
sick to my self hard work working inward.
(four colors azalean—don't forget it—distinct tart aftertastes.

        so then under what acid glare sequester my squalor-born
        deformed song body please sir don't
        kill me don't kill me sir please.
        w/just enough razor-slatch in levis crotch (now it's caught me/I cut
        wild left melrose blood surges turgid thru steel
        cockringd tight-thongd testes pufft-up high mass purple
        and early already danger-queen cruel   ripping
thru my shark skinnd night don't like shark skinnd but ripping, ripping

        manzanita manzanita sycamore locoweed creosote oak lone gray
            grebe grebe grebe grebe grebe grebe grebe grebe

running scared not much to fall back on throat dry to sing then
roots squirm upward roof of mother's ocean clutching song of
        terrified to tell you. how can I go on

rhythm-driven danger-queen M/B Club scurrying crotch to crotch, loud

dope music amyl stink boys' tongues hands all parts of me, dimlit sweat
narrow rooms boots crowds me kneeling surrounded eyebrows dripping
salt. terrified to sing me. how can I go on

umbilical cord word-jerkt, eyelid cells meshing in darkness, this song
      hates me, wants me to breathe its breath away, he moves away,
      leather-jacketed, tall, who won't speak, I follow him, hot room to
      hot room, sidling up, close to him, who won't even look my way, I
      beg him, this song, terrified, to grow, to be born, I beg him, he moves
      away, I follow, I whimper, I beg him

& my song is terrible for me this song burns a terrible no inside me whilst I write.
it cries out, not to have to dredge up hard-edgd cries, for me brutal, for me harsh, hates
      force, how can I force it, sing what I want, when I want, how can I go on,
      liar as craving it, liar as lusting for it, liar in the dark, see the needle,
      old man's cock, & see him pierce it, to see an old guy cry, & I beg him,
      do it to me too o do it to me too o please don't walk away o christ this song
      won't ever be born, doesn't want to be born, & how can I go on

manzanita manzanita sycamore locoweed creosote oak lone gray
           grebe grebe grebe grebe grebe grebe grebe grebe

once my son dying late prayer dream I'm 9 years old in our old
      black jalopy   my dad
dead, dead in the front-seat in a black
      overcoat   my mom
      invisible   drives us
to my movies in my night-
time not on any road but high up, out
      in my sky where meteors
      shine thru her I lean
forward   between them my baby my son his gaze his gaze
      sunk in time in my night-
time daddy daddy he's dying my dad wakes up to
touch the tip of a finger to my baby's
chest I whimper I wail out loud my december
      gusts sing thru
      busted out windows my tatterd up-
holstery flaps crazy in wind
              stream my teeth
chattery hey what theayter we goin at what movie what
      movie we gunnasee once we git there see the glow

from my laughy live son late prayer dream
light my frozen dashboard my whole jalopy fiery how we blaze clear, clear
out here in my wilderness   onward   onward

o   to nothing, no not
to nothing to
this this is this, what
alone my lone this is, great beyond
lazy wild sky in my fingertip, right ring
buried bunkbed splinter dad gouges my blood of nightly, for
me, & licks for me speechless, dis-
figured flesh-sign worried with a needle o, how many sun
downs dad got us down we awestruck divine we go to? I sing
this yr one poor gift for lack of one better my scar my gully
& way-gone 34 orbits later, tell   re-tell   o

o   this is no
saxophone solo dad but I can sing I can make it
all, yr frycook cuss wingspan riveter teethsuck flat times flat
broke ball-peen clawhammer crosscut bevel, level,
plane, make it all & yr odd sharp stare past me thru
lost Bakersfield Calif shack sunbeam dust
past forsook Nebraska farther back alone dad I can make it all
well, with my tremolo learnt in school sweet & high
to yr sapphire birthstone beltbuckle knuckles long blond eye
lashes clear up there on a peace   ful sum   mers eve   ning when
the sun   HAS   set don't bury me with you dad don't
bury me with you don't   o

at 26 in 61 noon yet void seeps in yet noon my noon years
        solitary without second
nights I delve inward tensions remember breath cry deep joints un
        fold thru street mist from hunger here,
inchoate, male snake of the time, I, void rain-seep
        steep down arroyos steaming junctures my
seven tectonic plates of soul on bed edge in heat of
        hotplate in stink of crackt boots drying I
dream again under Beckett & Faulkner in flame-bait or rain-drunk
        rooming-house cell/selma at mccadden
place/parkinglot now next-door cell alcoholic fat man fright
        at dim hall's lost end two

brittle greatgrandmothers fright
dying so quickly waking up slow to cold untold inside;
skinny guys with angry-cock acne, suckt off because lonely motor
        cyclists from corner hot
dog stand tight-butt young marines grimy in slept-in
        civvies I pose naked at my
window pulse grounded in headlight
glow drivers shivering hardup past incessant disintegrations of
        music muscle my years go,
        way I slay my blue temple/ weird, weird
waverings of my subtle body

running scared not much to fall back on throat dry try to sing then
    gunning to climax on melrose, again on my old meat lookout my song snares
    no one no one on robertson sidestreets 4 a.m. strung-out on fair

fax erratic on santa monica chugging slow past corners boy hitch
        hikers fresh gashes fleshflashing take me take me nowhere no one no one
        in tradesman dark back-alley my lights out & on selma heads shaking no no one on
        sunset; on vine, on vine, bedraggled, unshaven, one un

smiling one & my hands tremble breath races eyes glaze over you going far? not
        far I cut wild left from the right lane thru red light sudden siren
        shrieks I pull over fast o shit man he moans oh man fuck this here shit man
        ready to cry, we wait frozen thru the make on us, they drag him out,
        handcuff him, you want me to call anyone? no man no one head bowed ready to
        kill I gun off to song climax nowhere on no one & how can I go on

        manzanita manzanita sycamore locoweed creosote oak lone gray
            grebe grebe grebe grebe grebe grebe grebe grebe

wilderness onward onward I'd die to
        go into that forest & never come out what did
        you say Hank says I say I
said I'd die to hide in this forest/I see her in a sudden
drizzly clearing   visions you ache for & ache you, they
gnaw rake wrench split you & carve you in they gnaw, stock-
        still, torn skirt bleak sweater boots &
gusty about her in mazy twilight her dying eyelids lift
        toward the downrush glide
        of the solitary
raven swooping deep into wet glittery aspen shadows she holds

armload of dampt kindling whitehaired Slave Indian crone & children
　　　　run past her into the hut with kindling
& the rain, whispery upon her somber face she burns
rigid toward gray over ancient glade my bus roars by I
twist in my seat to see her buried under branches how they
　　　　thicken between us & cover her
　　　　how I cover her here in my interior
grave her gaze motionless toward gray her raven winging within me
　　　　thru rain spray chill in last
pure wonder & now: Hay River, Old Town, on this cold
　　　　southern shore

o　　　& jagged from lockheed & bitter　　　hisses
belt out of belt loops　　　lashes ass often　　　how I
must cringe　　　hate　　　breathe in in
secret　grow nervous ecstatic Hidden　　　set fire
to ladybugs　　　weep　　hurt fat girls　　　weep　　seek boys to
scorn me　　　dig in my dark my shovel snaps breast
bones　& how out loud wd I shout it　　shout it out
fierce　whip me dad whip me whip me til he crumples　& caves
in　　　in me　　whimpers Sonny　scat far you go task what lights
of yr catechisms　　whip you　　　task barren
trees　　barren skies　　whip you　　　task any
sad　　　wrong　　　old　　road　　beat you & wail
all yr poets Hidden son I nail my breath door tight & still　　　o

song: rude poetics black levis white windbreaker way past last-call
　　　　song: beginningless ignorance, sprung
　　　　from american warlike childhood meek
under hollywood streetlights brakescreech searchlights cops or harsh
cold shoulders in shadow'd alleys subtle body sung low as I slide
　　　　quick to my knees on glistening
pavement by wet thornbush, beginningless ignorance under my
　　　　tongue my shut eyelids my
far-in young thunders growling tense smoking hunting atremble on
corners says no says no say yes yes yes, coward of not
　　　　climbing to my song's peak way I
　　　　slay my blue temple, neons
sputter mad against sunrise remember my phone number call me, call me;
　　　　at 26 in 61 tiresian set-up hidden
underlife flare-up sleek night-jag idling as grinned-at Leland gets
　　　　in next to undreamt-of

proud blond messenger urgent demands disorder him abrupt to his
          eyes fierce beauty how it doth leap
Leland up rickety stairway selma at mccadden with his sudden one,
          beginningless ignorance how it doth lock
world-door after them Leland flicks lamp off they stand
          alone mute unknowing beginningless
ignorance how it doth scare

& my song is terrible for me this song churns a terrible no inside me whilst I write.
          speeding on hollywood boulevard furious before dawn tidal wave thrashing
          walls of mother's ocean when my head dies down I can feel it

then screech-halt last-chance underage thumb-out gee thanks for the lift mister
          wrinklefaced scragglehaird hunchback shiverer in a lost workshirt
          scrawny pale-neckt fear-pitcht stutterer hyperactive eyebrows & hand-wrencher,
          so then I drive gentle, I croon slow, lovingly, until he nods yessir, okay sir
          & then shift into low cruel danger-queen quiet, frightening our misted hills

& where sycamore locoweed creosote sleep & liveoak guards owl & deer, here, take my hand
          whispering, stumble him up overgrown paths soakt weeds chin-high
          trap him in a shadow of branches when my head dies down will I feel it
          take me out of here, o god, let me go, you do what I want, yessir, okay sir
          when my head dies down can I heal it, hide his clothes on hillside
          stark white humpback trembling, tidal wave thrashing on shores of mother's
          ocean, what do you think you're doing sir o what are you doing sir

hunchback in my song under hard belt-blows, pleading, obeying all warnings,
          deformed song body, writhing, choking, gritting his teeth thru song-beat,
          please don't sing of me, please don't sing of me, on hands knees crawling,
          slipping, twisting thru brambled rhythms, stop, stop, what are you doing,
          dust made mud by dew streaking his body original terror in his hoarse
          young cry please don't kill me sir o please don't kill me sir & my
          whole wild hill shrills fire

I drop my belt, he stands there shaking, is it over? is it all over? wasn't it real?
          no, kid, playacting, joking, playacting, begins to cry & I hold him, this song
          hates me, wants me to stifle its life away, safe/unsafe his terrified way,
          doesn't want to be born or sing of me in dirt near azalea branches, sick to my
          self, hung-over, breaking, tearing, swallowing my bright pure petals & I
          wonder is it over, I curl up on earth under flowers, I wonder, is it all
          over?

    & pinkster & cardinal & salmon-rose & snow;
        & how can I go on;
    & curld 38-yr-old foetal position ear to my dry ground crying;
    & bitter azalea tiresian song;
        & how can I go on;

& morning squeezes forces me thru crevice unto glare so then I lift
    my deformd song body to my blue sun risen low
    over turbulent horizon slow motion explosion lone gray
    grebe grebe grebe grebe grebe grebe grebe grebe;
& how can I go on;
    & pinkster & cardinal & salmon-rose & snow;
    & how can I go on

toward cold southern shore, forest dusky
    trails muddy, icy
    scud, low sunrays slat I listen for
    source sound enfold guide me to my-
self, hide me in the, at first far-off frail
    moan in my spine, Hank
leads on running soon spruce & aspen thunder the
    rumbling en-
    gulfs me some-
thing beyond convulsive suffers seethes
    rages in itself, Hank
    bolts forward, breaks
    thru my final
    trees I am pulled, skulled
thru my wrench Woven-Here down stark hard sand Great Slave
    Lake's gnarled uprushing roar
shudders daemonic its groan thru me my night sun-
    light gleams blood-rust on my waves, gleams
off floating tree-hulks far out adrift sinking &
    heaved huge black in
slow moiling cry wind squalls sand, leaves, over weatherbleacht tree-
    trunks washed up on
shore ragged roots flare gaunt against lightning I gaze I gaze
    long into my night how lost my light goes

o   one blond slim 1949 dad's one solid stunnd
noonburnd carpenter on his own poor man's plumbd
redwood rooftop beveld & groind against one gruff song
from our longwinded sky in a glare under far blue sun
who stonefaced stares down at a boy
skinny & scribbling at the wheel of the stalld black jalopy those harsh
hardond mystical clear
groans got forgotten whose unclear
glance flashes breathtaken high
into his breathtaking higher up enemy's eye & both do remember
that ocean in their brains where it rains forever. only as long
as one quick flare wch fire flings slick down his naked spine
that the man wrenches back to hammer & shinglestack,
& the boy in the black wreck falls back to his fresh black song   o

PAINT CHILD AT PAIN AT SHOCK AT

blood run down thorn down greeny skin
white gold indigo big plaster mom
    with pearls for tears & dad's
glass eyes gleaming in stained light &
    doll's teeth glistening in
    agonies of twisting Jesus
under bluesky ceiling's high tiny electric stars.
    bless me father for I have sinned: I

stick out my peter in firstgrade naptime
show it to Timmy it's so stiff it's so red his
eyes pop wide you dope you dope   recess rings I
scat scared down the steps he's telling the guys
he's telling the jump-ropers ummmm they ummmmm
    pouting their upper lips
    over their lowers
Eddy shouts LET'S GO BEAT HIM UP pigtails
    flick squeal giggle don't
touch him he's nasty but they chase me clear
where the skinny lindens by the sixthgrade swings are
    Eddy spits on my arm Timmy & Neil
Kirk & Dean yell dopey you dopey you crummy stupid
    recess rings   I go choking
slow thru spiderwebs of mean beady eyes.
Leland did you do what Timmy says you did? & a
    glister of bracelets
    pierces the storyroom

yes I nod yes & are you sorry & I nod yes
    Miss Lacy's locket
    glints gold on my face
Leland will you promise me not to play nasty?
    & I nod yes   now promise the children
I won't ever play nasty I swear to the storyroom.

        storyroom. storyroom. o
            wind mow the hairs back.
            toy shovels going rust, wormheart
            thudding. sky, go to sleep. I'm
            I'm just afraid. dustmotes snuck.
            leaping cockleburs. make me good.

this your body & blood? white
butterfly. cobweb. treedust sun-
light. storyroom. storyroom.

    Louie's a marine he mows down Japs
     he swings me around by my heels too
my daddy drives
    the rattletrap pickup & I scrunch hard
low in Louie's lap
    that bunchup in his levis is a grownup pecker
he hooks his tough arm out the window the wind
    mows all the hairs back
he hooks my white arm on top of his brown arm
    okay leatherneck c'mon let's
    both hook our arms out
    I scrunch lower & Louie
swings me around I can see tough eyes
well Lee I do declare
    your little boy here
      is tryin' to feel my dingus.
o wind mow the hairs back. bad Japs die.
well Lee I do declare
    your little boy here
      sure is hot stuff o
wind mow the hairs back & bad Japs die.

    one day we dig in the hole daddy dug
    to plant the plumtree I find a long
    earthworm slimy gray with wet pink
belly close your eyes Punkie open your mouth I
    dangle it in, it wriggles
    on his tongue his chin Bobby
shrieks don't close your mouth o don't close your mouth
o my little baby brother you got a worm in your mouth
    Punkie wails, my brother Johnny
    hits me with a stick you meanie you
    meanie Bobby
shouts   come on Punkie   let's go
    home Johnny
    hits me & hits
    me meanie damn meanie damn meanie.

ditch damp & shitdark, blind cold tails
slippery by my cheeks my bare
butt sinking in loam & I whisper:
Bobby bury me Billy bury me throw
   dirt on my knees Bobby wet
   clods on my dick Billy let
me have dirt on my chest my face I'm
magic I can breathe underground.
but their mommy calls them in & they go
but their mommy calls them in & they go
see their toy shovels going rust in the sun
cloudshift burning over everyone & no
   one to shovel dirt on me down
here where I sing in my shitdark my
wormheart thudding out bury me & bury
me I'm magic I can breathe underground.

across Lake Street   high backyard weeds I
   pull down my pants   Travis stares
I take off his glasses I can't see give me my
glasses back take off your pants no give me my
glasses first take off your pants no mother will
   see us the
     weeds hide us he
       starts to. Travis Travis we
pull up our pants fast Travis get
in here this instant don't play with that nasty
boy. lying still breathing weeds watching sky go
to sleep go to sleep his
   voice thru the screendoor his
   glasses gone sunset: my mother says go
home now Sonny it's getting dark: my mother says go
   home Sonny Hickman it's dark.

mommy is he everywhere he is everywhere
mommy is he inside us he is inside us
   & does he see everything o
Sonny does he ever & when the time comes
   make a list of all your badthoughts
   make a list of all my badthoughts
   make a list of all bad actions
   make a list of my bad actions &

tell them to the priest but mommy I'm afraid
silly Sonny what are you afraid of? I'm
    I'm just afraid.

it's secret now but not for always Jerry &
    me barefoot on canal path my
    jiggling my arm on his neck he
leans into me freight train's roar,
shivers clean up your toes to your stomach don't it? still
here in this shack beside me those dustmotes snuck
    up thru white lashes he's
    looking up to me over &
over our hands in white waistbands, Jack
Armstrong is on I've never done that can I I
    stick up for him to mean
    teachers loan him my sling-
shot, save him from badboys, can I I
slink to my knees now. he won't tell.
pretty little prick some lint in the wrinkles.
pretty little prick some lint in the wrinkles.
pretty little prick some lint in the wrinkles.

& if I could climb into Jerry's eyes I'd
look down on my headtop I'd feel how
    I do what he don't I
roll this here cookie in my asshole he
watches me watching him munch it his
    eyes in mine if
I could breakthrough to his green eyes I'd
taste my own ass in that cookie. if
I could be locked up in his dog eyes I'd
    follow along Lake
Street, leashed thru my buttons my wide
blue eyes full of me. don't pull so damn
    hard damn you damn
string hurts my thing, Sonny
Hickman leads me along Lake Street past eleven front yards: let's go see
Ralphie Ralphie's five he's dumb & does it.
there in the vacant lot weeds Ralphie's
    in his broken
wagon playing pilot,
dropping bombs: Sonny wants you to do it to him you'll do it won't you

Ralphie? Ralphie nods, dumb German pilot.
so Sonny takes his rockhard thing out
    in plain daylight,
look there's old man Murphy
watching from his frontporch rockingchair: so what Sonny says c'mon do
it Ralphie & Ralphie does boy he's dumb.
Sonny's sunburnt nose drips sweat his eyes
    shut, open, go
soft go wide go hard get
mean he jerks away he spits see his spit dribble off Ralphie's chin?: poor
Ralph dumb Ralph, scared in his German cockpit.
you're nasty Sonny laughs you'll go to
    hell. Ralphie cries
flat on the floor of his
wagon. yanked by my string, leaping cockleburs: I'll see ya Ralphie &
dumb Ralphie's banging his head back screeching.

what're you so scared to tell the priest don't
cry Sonny I won't scold you there now there you did
    what with who with Bobby &
    Billy yes & at school I
did it Miss Lacy sent me to the prin-
cipal there now there don't cry just say you
committed an act of impurity how many
    times I never counted don't
    cry count them for the priest it
'll be fine oh Lee I just don't know he
cried so he's done those filthy things don't you
think we should punish him well Eleanor if you
    think so well Lee I just don't
    know. come in here Sonny kneel
by your bunk drop your pants but daddy why
your mother says you've been a nasty boy
with Ralphie & Jerry daddy but mommy but
    me no buts son drop your pants
    kneel by your bunk & count 'em.

I missed mass four times I was late five what
else I told lies how many times I don't
remember I was mean to my brothers I pre-
    tended the altarboys &
    priest was naked I put a
earthworm in Punkie's mouth I was sorry

what else I wet the bed my mommy says
nine times what else & I & I committed uh
      an act of impurity
      by yourself or with others
with both with little girls no with little
boys how many times I think six father
yes my son what else father I yes don't cry i
      couldn't wait in the dark I
      went in my pants all over.

dear Jesus they're asleep but I'm praying
this is my dog Tiny chewing my knee
didn't I see Hail Mary smiling when I said
      penance my mother says I
      made it up she's mad I wet
my pants will I be in heaven when you're
in my mouth what will you taste like sliding
down my throat that's my stomach growling I'm sorry
      won't I be too rotten to
      swallow you if I have bad
dreams tonight stop that Tiny I won't bite
you just let you melt it's bedtime Sonny
Jesus save me from my badboys make me good amen.

      this your body & blood?
      closed eyes I
kneel at your altar head tilting backward my
      tongue peaks
now you're a white butterfly my lips caught
now you're a cobweb stuck to my teeth in a dream
can my tongue nudge you so you won't shatter
wake up I want you to love me
      so I can rise
elbows & knees pure dust in a sun-
ray, come in thru my throat so my lies die
      come down let me swallow
you, so my daddy my mommy both see
you, my grandma, Johnny & Tiny all see
      you in Sonny Sonny in Sonny.
      savior in-
side me glued to the roof of my mouth I hear
      you cry
Sonny Sonny Sonny Sonny my skin

in shivers Tiny waggy in our old car in
me Johnny grabs my rosary mommy
stoops to straighten snagged stockings in
    me grandma her
facepowder-smudged easter-blue Ethel
Barrymore glove just-so to her cheek, veil
    snared on an earring in
me watching people gab thick treedust sun-
light look look my daddy yellow hair slicked back—
    stony into me & stony back,
    this my body my blood.

        my body my blood my body. plum-
            tree in icysharp wind. foxhole
            dirt. stiff fire. a forehead of secrets,
            like a dirtclod slung at you & a rock in it,
            blurring past the torn screendoor.
            enemy windows. birdwing dumbclucks.
            sleepwarm skin so moongray sweaty.
            mommy, what's a nitwit? hush, hush, my
        blood my body my body my blood.

East Bakersfield winters trees strip & go
    dusty-blank, the sky
    oilsmoke-
blank, vacant lot foxtails sick white ochre.
in my enemy foxhole dusk and eye on
    Mrs. Landers' windows I
gouge dirty words out of sticky ground they
    cuss up black thru sandcrust.
    PISS   PECKER   ASSHOLE   SHIT.
mommies get disgusted to run to the outhouse
shivering past the plumtree in icysharp wind on
    wet planks over mud
    & scared
to be seen outdoors torn blue bathrobe flapping.
in my enemy foxhole dirt I spit for
    Eddy who spat on my arm got
hit on his bike by a truck his arm cut
    off whole block of blood
    PISS   PECKER   ASSHOLE   SHIT.
mommies get headaches in cold & in heat.
mean in enemy foxhole I press naked peter

into black dirt, grind
asscheeks
stab in bared crumbly blockprint my name.
Eddy you chased me you called me a stupid &
    I hope you're in deepdown hell.
Mrs. Landers windows blaze I scramble
    into my overalls shaking
    ERASE   ERASE   ERASE   ERASE.
mommies get sad & say damn it to hell too much
    mommies mad being mommies.

& I fool them sleeping until they're asleep I
tiptoe thru the shack to the flickering front-
room I kneel before the gurgling gas
heater I stare until my eyes melt,
redorange greenblue, until they're burnt white as
whispers, I lower ragged peejays I lean
closer on my knees as close as I can
until heat singes my new brown hairs & I
swell up so redhot I can't stand it my
pisshole's crying almost in blisters & I
scrunch burning near boiling until I'm
not Sonny anymore not Sonny not Sonny I'm stiff fire
    trembling & terrible & tall I
crackle & hiss in my scarlet great flame.

darnit Dickie Lyons let's get naked in
Mrs. Landers' chickencoop I don't want to
Dickie Lyons come on in this chickencoop
Sonny you're nasty you ain't a Catholic
I'll hit you Dickie I'll make you get naked
Sonny you're crazy I am not you are so:
crazy dummies strip in stinky chickencoops.
darnit Dickie Lyons I saw you get stripped
last night I climbed up that castorbean tree out-
side your window I saw you in hot water
I peeked clear into your bathtub I saw you
puttputting your boats & rubbing your peter
Sonny you're crazy I am not you are so:
crazy dummies climb trees to see in bathtubs.
daddy told me what you crazy dummies want
you want everybody nasty just like you

& that's always what you're trying out on me
when you get naked in front of me with your
head thru your knees & your butthole in the air
Sonny you're crazy you better be careful:
crazy dummies just freeze up that way & die.

toesink in powdery. cattail feathers drifty.
   afternoon canal a
deep breath unwinding a long ghost story & tall
sunreeds slat dayfall on my skin.
   waterflash downaways.
a forehead of secrets floats under the roadbridge its
   glint eyes seek me the current
grips quick cold tight to my chest, holds still.
   & he swims closer.
he disappears. he's nearby underwater. mud
   tugging at me
clambering out slipping backward. slender wrists
dripping. my breath harsh on the slope.
   his tense white body
streaks twisting into air & his blond hair bullets
   stinging loud half-circle spray.
water laps his muscled waist he flicks snot off his nose,
   squints up at me.
what's the matter little boy I scare you?
   low & rough & his
laugh like a dirtclod slung at you & a rock in it.
come on back in the canal kiddo
   I won't hurt you
come on back in the water here's a big surprise.
   holds his swimtrunks in the air, grinning.
come on. what do you say? cat got your tongue?
   he squats in the water
only his sunburnt whisper calling scaredycat
   scaredycat
come on in so I can shove big dick in your face
you can't suck me off from up there on that bank.
   I stare. he frowns.
look how I made a big surprise for you kid.
   lifts up his hand, wet brown in it.
see I shit you a big hard turd. catch. I duck. he
   laughs, sinks backward.
& disappears. swimming underwater. I wait.

waterflash downaways.
his blond hair floats into roadbridge shadows. gone.
the sky is darker now the ashen canal
    wraps me in dusk I
stand where he stood both hands plunged in swimtrunks.
    seeing nothing. staring in muddy
swirl. tiny raindrops sharp on my shoulders, black
    pockmarks dent
breeze-rippled waterskin. I hope you come back I
hope you come back. still standing still
    where he stood.
toesink in powdery. current colder, stiffer.
    twilight canal a
gray breath unhushing a long ghost story & tall
moonreeds slat nightfall thru my hair.

chugging home from the movies in our old jalopy can't
stop at Tip's for hamburgers our daddy's broke, rattle up
    wet dirt drive to weatherbeaten shack & mommy
buries her face in pasted-on fingernail hands she cries
oh I can't take anymore I can't take anymore we're
always broke you never make any money look at this
    junkheap oh Lee I can't live here I just can't I
can't even remember why I married you sometimes I
don't even know why. daddy stops the car in darkness to
touch her she pulls away oh don't do that but honey he
    whines & she pushes broken handle & stumbles
to the porch, plump pretty legs under crumpled cotton skirt
blurring past the torn screendoor & our daddy runs after
    her & nobody turns any lights on.

out of the nightsea where I can fly
    high above cottonwoods
awake in the shack grandma dreams in &
    brothers I
creep from bedbunk sneak to doorscreen dare-
devil in peejays on the lean-to stoop to my slow heart-
    beat stripping.   then in
joy in nakedness in bright in dark
stark ice luna all in my chest crackt, hair
    fretted thru pitchblack by castorbeans.
panting at roots burrs milkweeds thistles I
sprint shack's grass, leap earth berm, bare feet

sink into still warm tar of Lake Street & hush:
go snickers from enemy windows hush
go birdwing dumbclucks from dirtyards hush I
    poke my white boner at the moon,
    starglints on boyass I bend to
bless the old road with my tongue to bless
    elfpricks going stiff into secrets the
faraway dogyelps go hush, they go hush.
    then run then I run
back to the little house under its grim
    cloudskin I'm snug in, no griefstricken
grandma eyelids twitching me sorry or angry.

    I worry what's a nitwit. hot
    day alone in shack & brothers
    gone playing, daddy mommy rivet
    bomber tailfins in warplant.
    see me dancing bareassed on chairs
    hear me sing these low words loud.
    I knot rope on hardon dash outdoors
    loop plumtree branch I jerk I
    leap I swing silly & sparkling
    yellow plums soft pellet me. I
worry what's a nitwit. Johnny says, we're
off on a trip. where to? mommy says,
never mind. give this to your father.
daddy daddy, mommy & Johnny ran away. he
reads & bang goes his fist & he drags me
to Mrs. Willis. Sonny, stay overnight with
David & I climb into David's damp bed.
I gaze at bony ribcage rise, fall, sleepwarm
skin so moongray sweaty. in kidsnore,
inch by inch slithering under shushthin
sheet until held breath hovers over
kidstink pajamaflap & my stretcht tongue
quivers, feathertipt, tickles kidsalt.
he stirs he sleeps, these brave cubscout
lips slip soft-snapdragon-tight on
wiggleless pollywog, sweetpea-pale,
hairless, nutless. I sneak to the pillow.
    David asleep. mouth open. moist
    blue eyelids. blind. still.
    I worry what's a nitwit. daddy called

that tall skinny guy who grabbed me in the city-
     park swimmingpool toilet one. mommy
     what's a nitwit? Sonny hush.
     stop dwelling on it but daddy said
a nitwit's brain's gone vomitsour son it's been
screwed in sideways upside down then his eyes went
     thinslittery.
     nitwits go after boys from swimmingpools
they grab you from behind when you're peeing their sharp
     fingernails pinch into your shoulders
     they choke you their thick elbows
     go around your throat & lift you they
yank your hair to make you stiffen they gurgle
the big world's dirty words & squeeze you tight you
     can't even squirm.
     nitwits get fun from little boys crying
they never have any friends & they want to stick
     their grownup peckers in you they get
     mad if you say I'm only
     nine years old it'll hurt me they get
mad if you promise instead to lick it they
almost shout that won't hurt enough & you don't
     know what to do.
     Sonny hush. stop dwelling on it. you hear?
nitwits never like to look scared of you they hate
     swimtrunked boys yelling daddy mommy
     they can't hear you I saw them
     they're still in the swimmingpool no they're
right outside they'll come kill you if I yell hard
nitwits' bugeyed faces get sad they let you
     alone then they
     skedaddle. after a while you can come
out careful in sunshine skittery thru branches
     you can lean on a strong tree & breathe
     slow so pretty soon you start
     hearing everything plain again like
those high-up breezes thru jittery leaves &
those way-high-up screams the little kids scream on
     teeter-totters.
     Sonny hush. stop dwelling on it. you hear?

Fort Providence on the Mackenzie River

& about how lost my light goes & about
cruelty my contemporary, about my way things are, about
my first eerie view of my lake hay river deserted september trembling,
tiresias sleepless raging from my malevolent lake, & about gross
cruelty to my song, my way thing are my contemporary, about these
climates strange fauna, what my line strains forward, giant
ravens motionless gaunt at my forest's black edge guarding
my oracular writhen lake under rain—small stark hope
from moribund hinterground wrenching my anger toward stabs of the
lightning, loveless grim roar my furious lake my sunset about
about what I have handcufft, about
what I have tortured, about
what I have severed the songs of I don't

dream anymore know where it's going great slave lake
sang me go down & go down, stand still in my thunder & hear it,
slasht tongues of vision scream far into dark. no death.
no death a strong dark a sun-trip a burning a sweeping, strict
pitch dark, all of it, & no death, no death, fire
flow, stars, quake hot, leaves of my nightmare, quiver!
I want to see all of it happen, I want my blue sun breath door wide open, I want
inevitable spreading joke & disease, white noise from my flute, gray soft
hairs of his damp perineum brusht against eyelids soundproof room rust-red
sand lake's edge at last ray flickering deep into my long tender blind
sinuous tremulous grasses no merciless ending tó it
& about how far off omega & about how much yet undetected
strangeness, scion of
naked charm, blue sun breath—symmetry's gasping child a river a calm
power listlessly overcast subarctic heavens restless, hesitant
rain my buried song drumming synaptic explosion flow no
merciless ending tó it & dying dying to continue ache-
ing, riverbarge now groaning my old bus over, & I here grippt on deck for
revelation downriver, tiresias river, striving oracular shapeshifting
rasa-river, huncht here tight against waterdrops, whipping in
wind long hair overcoat focust on risk what will be about bright
languages, bred of ravens rivertongues black galaxy'd gnats in my sun-
clash, & husht under fugue of the forest, where song—
song shivers

apprehensive rasa-risk open to numinous ill process or blue
            temple be wounded grum void seep in/
shapeshifter tectonics mnemonics beginningless ignorance high over snake
            bed I go back headlights streak ceiling at 26 in
61 tremble before him begin being child until I am all child, whisper my
            questions reach thru dark to touch on tiptoe to kiss
him whisper my questions, why he will not speak or move, why he
            shoves me away, turns to my
window street wet below says do what I want falls
            mute cold beginningless
ignorance waits, repeats, do what I want, I whisper, tell me, as cars
            shiver slow past numinous
            ill process his young
gruff words seep in where strength flails where doubt fucks temple down, wind-
breaker T-shirt boots black levis sweet naked for this guy my
            pale elbows dirty knees, dumb-
struck, shoulderblades helpless begun being child all child all
            child lie down on yr bunk I do I lie down;
uprush song temblor for this strippt song Leland as
fierce lordly beauty coming my way flicks lamp on, stay
            still stay quiet under breath under
            cold wild narrowing gaze be
ginningless ignorance how it doth quake me
& then into dung to be heavend I was ever thralld, & to plunge my
            swollen voice
thru this black hole inside me wherein each song
's compacted made dense melodious my last
            song my first I alone
sing, hello now let me tempt stranger I need I need, come
            quick & he does come, he does
                        come
                    young
                        so strong
                                wrenching
            my world's wet innocence out
of his body all wrappt in bronze muscle he is music he is singing:

            how well it is I am not afraid. & how well I am
            not afraid, not afraid. & how well it is I am not afraid.

now, show me my blue-lippt children stilld & curld on the stone teat.

            not afraid.   & he is music.   not afraid.

cd shed rage
shd love come.

however he come:
      in suntanned form of whore with navyblue flight bag
      fills, takes, orders, wearing sneakers or barefoot
      kisses hugs suckles, believable with the bullwhip, reasonable
      rates, dope not included, or

in moonlit widow's form, Jeanne, hesitant, delicate under the black
      nightfall cascading down her shoulders & her back,

         unafraid.   & she is music. unafraid.

         cd shed rage
         shd love come.

now, show me my embarrassing ones my despised ones my troubled ones.
      I've come to burst the death skin off you.

o, hopeful & attentive sentences: forever. sunshine acid penetrates
      nerves, upflutters those amorous high
      emberd leaves amberd clouds out there, where my
      shrieking kindless blvd weaves, & I spy him:

crossing calm against traffic to command this tremulous this exultant door/ worried
      uncertain
      narcissistic nostrils, eyebrows, serious
      eyes/ much more

than ever I have hope for: man, man,
      shivering & afraid at cold summer's cold eyes. older these
      hungrier fantasies unsnarld & writhe
      on the floor, at yr feet, where you stare,

on earth, with form & with affliction.
or, Jeanne sing my newborn song in New York to the spring skies, then!

resuffering my journal of winter '64, callow
perplexities this second symbolling flower
blossoms to memorialize, whether it fold shut

112

or unwithering open out, or never in time
uncover any human crying
not alive yet & never embraced alive. sometimes
my Ginny is in it, evolving thru thralldoms inseeing & scrying.
prophesying seven years safe without confusion,
& sometimes someone calling himself Leland is in it, gathering
his fluttering lights into complex
patterns, magnifying intensities until they shatter.
up against it, in camera/on camera, irredeemable, no rare
frailest santarasa, no gentlest human high & my whole way inward dying/ where
did he fuck up how did he go
wrong, huh; as merciful the snow
buried their dark apartment where they feared
to touch & to dream & to sing from the gasping source. o,
sothsegger, sothsegger scry, snow
compassions from my sky on their mute small weird. & absolve them.
for then! one spring & summer, sweet widow Jeanne my muse/ or now
            was his name Brian? grins, steps clean of his clothes—

When you have been fuckt by so many hundreds of darknesses
So many summery fusions over the crumbled sill, receiver of
Stolen goods a key to the brain's room
                                    o little piggy-piggy,
You run for the high devastations fires pursue & the harsh wind
favors. & not getting it sung. not getting it sung. she was
here during the early songs with her black silken hair she
                                    greeted them smiling,
tentative understandings & solemn, restless days with Milton & twilight, her hazel
gaze far out the window
over April's brash hustle, motherly & perplexd, minding
                                    my silence.

just syllables
cd make us touch
fingertips.
                        & her son waits also for her
when I arrive to wait for her, evenings
invading, will not
nod from his rockingchair, slight, 16 yrs old
& bright, bright kind of a
mathematical wizard Jeanne whisperd/
                                    chaos of citysounds up

from that 14th st subway stop one flight below is all there is between us,
      uttering no word in the dark.
& I can neither speak nor fear not to ache to hold me to him like a,
father.
               together, Solomon, this way, we wait
for her, while whatever harmony or song has wrencht me here, to yr
grim hurt, you hate, & hate
this yr first lonely place in my song where Jeanne my muse yr mother
leans smiling down to you/
               & she kisses yr hair

               cd shed rage
               shd love come.

almondblonde bitter lost, hidden hurt city sucks dirt to her,
slush shit to her, sooty cruise
smut to her, swollen lonely sweater shy tight pale
brave curve of her, defiled on the I.R.T.
o Ginny, my Ginny,
defiant-jawed shoulders tensed makeup caked, eyes
front, brittle dreams final & early all dead-
set against toughness break-
down, dazed visions, occult scars
from her burning sojourns thru unbreathable fires a-
blaze in her last hope crystal,
scrying, bewildered,
cantaloupes, oranges, mildewed, rotting,
dark ceiling unswept, heavy cobwebs swaying, in
enchantment by sorrowing yarrow stalks, star
charts tarot deck ouija board scam channels unto grace & forgetting how
strongly she wept, what blindly she fled from, why one stark song she feared, o
sothsegger, sothsegger scry, snow
solace from my sky on her mute dim weird/ & absolve, absolve her.

or do I sing it wrong, Jeanne, when will I sing it right?
all of it effortful: how I break away; how I disappear;
how I vanish; how I abandon you; forget you; fall

mute as these long summer hours we spend wordless, motionless,
each of us in wonderment, how to heal, how to mend
what no one has severd yet
               what no one has broken.

114

what no one has severd yet, & what no one has broken—

    I wd sing about—. but how my song
                              stops.

Aphroditos Phalanthos, come from the sea. come here to me.

Jeanne, Jeanne, why is my song of you dying, Jeanne,
       do our bodies betray us
       do they yield us bleak measure
       mock exultations, or violate shockingly
       faith-hummed litanies of union, or

by my window, Jeanne, yr reluctant thin body, moonlit,
& the blue elms asleep beyond it in the courtyard, or

       in pigeon-fluttering noon, on Bleecker,
       yr hands fly sudden to yr mouth to stifle
       some injurd ideal of the loneliness returning

       or Brian, in wrencht
convolutions of the emblem—Brian-Jeanne—also
afraid, unbuttoning his child-shirt a child-day, this
ritual not passion, as my words come halting, remorseful,
unwillingly to bed with me, his blond slow arms
       aching not to embrace these
memories of—how shd I name them, Phalanthos?—

       freshborn innocent songs
       left to cough & cry on a mountain?

    & I wd sing about—. but my song
                              stops.

shared, mean, low rent, shared
brownouts, & failures shared & those tender
sudden deteriorations of their distrust, gaps
in it, some laughter some wise
cracks, joints passed under lamentations of lady day, or else satie very sadly, he
leaning hard on her, so seeming true & teaching, commanding, go
easier on the eyeline dont scorch the pork
chops sweep the fucking crud out, take fonder

care of yr sick black dog, Ginny; she timid, she wild, casting
curious lame spells against her psyche to believe him, what's the
use of his hands on her use of his tongue in her use of his wrong
song in her dont want you to sleep here, please let me
sleep here, then sleep here, dont go, please, please, sleep here.
& to the piteous plaint of the mad outlaw declaring
benign acts of aggression on an unknown poetry, they did kiss & they did suck,
& they interlockt upon the bed, & on the floor, & up against the sill, biting,
huffing, & forct their dead false song as their dead truth leered. o,
sothsegger, sothsegger scry, snow
grieving from my sky on their lewd shared weird. & absolve them.

Aphroditos Phalanthos, come from the sea. come here to me.

& Charles, warm old friend, calls—you ought to go on with it, even
        so wounded a thing
& Bill calls—my friend Bill a poet—a tenderness
is in it. get on with it
Steve calls. I rail at my friend against my prison
Harry calls—Harry my friend a poet—aint the song
finisht yet, may I come for a visit?
& Juan calls—my friend Juan a poet—I must go to Spain
        I must go to Mexico
        I must find my lost father in the Philippines
        I must learn Spanish, I must search
        all my life I've tried to be *white*washt!
        my country's my prison, I must escape!

                cd shed rage
                shd love come.

my skin's my prison my body makes these wrong
                                    songs here

        of Brian whose body's one prison
by my bedside, in ritual sweat, belt grippt, folded, fisted
        with this ember-sear to punish the music, burnt
from my chest to my navel, done against sweet strange breathings, who gets
        paid & gets
        gone, vanisht
under shudders of palm leaves black against an aged-gold sullen great moon.

116

but what of the song, I lamented, & what of the rapture?
      & Jeanne, astonisht,
her soft cool hands on my forehead:
                   you mourn only

the sacred robin moaning at twilight from his brief spring tree.

     & I start to cry. & she hushes me.
     o, who can put the music back in that tree?

          cd shed rage
          cd shed rage
          cd shed rage

          shd love come.

internal estrangement betrayal stern river convulse
me; no welcome from my sacred wildness, about
this childish swoon state I exalt into manic dismay this
frenzied seeking along my blue sun river
for the "poetics of this situation not yet figured,"
I have to breathe one. about no power
to be heard thru my song
& what can I sing them, what can I bring them, build up my
work's queer fused rasa
love it hide it hate it uphold it, about
that old Slave Indian mending or caulking his boat by the river

a ministering cause to unlock the insoluble problems of the work
mending his boat by the river in my mind forever
& no glance nor any note of me taken
bald tiresian, early morning sun blinding off the water as I pass by, stifled.
& o which form direct action (what we sing abut will affect you.
o which form direct action, this weedsrabid graveyard
for transgressors of wilderness, three bright ravens above me,
& no glance nor any note of me taken for that I am unclean I have
dared set foot in his stillness because I have none; none.
my wise fierce river exaggerated, depths of my formidable
tangle of aspens & pines in gusty september exaggerated, giant gleaming
ravens exaggerated, exaggerated   my pale thin skin
in this isolated, luminous place

internal estrangement betrayal stern river convulse
me, o teach, wrong how I have gone, where, when wrong, I go,
living vulcanian riverlight, erupt & cry in me loving, break, break,
deepest cleanest seed   rhythms visions firm my
freshskinnd unlockt prayer: two tall, dusky-skinnd
Slaves, severe glances sullen sidelong, unspeaking (I
flail at these gusts of gnats, or of spirits, or
of their green gold weir their familiars/ who
pass me on this dirt narrow trail from their own sweet
proud village, who as if in despite of despising me stride
to their childhoods' river & launch their trim canoe,
cross calm marsh arm, beach on the far beach, young, strong,
shirts open, sleeves uprolld in cold over
muscular understandings, who squatting smoke & stare at me & I
am wrencht by iron-black broad-stretcht wings grace thru my chaos gliding
one long, sure, even-held breath streaking low over the water
vanishing into the gold-leav'd mystery, Providence
Island, & my hurt song, whimpers, wd follow, follow, my single
raven, wrong, wrong how I have gone, & where, when wrong, I do go

everpassing autos hum wet over street below sacramental
          process slips jacket off I lie
          in subtle husht boy-thin
body beneath numinous ill gaze under lamplight, undoes
cufflinks, tie, I reach out to touch, no you can never touch me, doffs
          shirt shoes socks unbuckles belt-
buckle my cock up bright o hoist me higher in my harsh malign for this
          ragged rasa for stern aloof beauty whose
tight black slacks inch low down slow over hard rock silence be
ginningless ignorance sprung music-muscle gleam-tippt at large & at
          lung top crowing all
          child all child all child; o
where there used to be sky after dust; dad, mom, off to their warplant;
          I wd lie all alone in tall temples of grass in
midnights of other songs. must be anyone sung in my fire. years gone,
          years go. fierce
beauty, above, below, behind, before, to my right, to my left, beyond, must be
          anyone song my door. lordly
beauty mute unmoving my hands can neither reach him nor touch
          my own subtle
body (stay hurt stay isolate under numinous ill process, flawd
          song, strippt child-cry
astounded exalted abased / obey

118

of Ginny, troubled, of
bewilderment his prophetess, in
dubiety uneasily, at noon & by candlelight,
trembling, scrying
imageries of neverwill as he watched her, terrified,
with sickness devouring his vision
& sickness oppressing his tongue,
unformed, isolate, in guilt of hid severance,
innocent of joy, escaping her,
fleeing into his future as he wrote it, into wept-for abysses,
svetaketu, plotinus, areopagite of the stammered nonnothing,
until a childhood arose in his throat & his blue sun breath door yielded
& his god of the bitter rasas descended to inseed him/ & he awoke.
as solstice-dawn neared, he cried,
self-moved, prophesying, his own vain seer,
of blind eyes, solitude, white serpents,
while beside him distant she listened to her lone stark song, & feared. o,
sothsegger, sothsegger scry, snow
consternations from my sky on his safe, cold weird/ & absolve, absolve him.

      forlorn in a severance rain from root,
then to slave austerely to wail down insanity into my singing rages
        pleading stop stop me enthralld
by avidyā's big boot death grum fugue death dry fountain death pig pouf
        turdblossom cringing anonymous slurp I
beg trappt braying hate me dont hate me this is my
        song, sourd in brutality & the acrid stench of.
        pale sweated eye-
brows strong Lion transfixing me: growling slamming home bosst dim citizen this
        busted vainglorious maleficent fugitive choke-fuck.
& Lion he rears fierce in me somebody watch watch us a steely true blue
badgd snig maybe   & divine right Lion he roars suck & I wail my
        whole song down clear to my snuff-flick lone
some getting off grand last passions over my long dead tongue my own Lion & my
                                      [own brutish law.
      forlorn in a severance weed from rain,
a god I am & mine own slave so far have I faked me repetitive cold
        arrests sully me fast, once
spread darks about me before I cd figure, & devouring afteraborts narrow
        awake knobbykneed paunchy grayhaird in scrub
        oaks, redfaced stumbling
dry path to dry creek bed to lurk a long naked kneeling morning hidden

                    dastard under thick blackwillow in
                    shitsong in self wallow I
beg you beat me let me swallow you & strict eyes of my Lion please search me
                                                                how to kill.
                    this furious beating beggd,
                    judgd abject we go,
daredevil Lee & Lion tailgating, los feliz western la brea gardner, scatter my
            limits, boundspreadeagled, drunken, druggd, gaggd. home.

of Leland his
fraudulence, in shame of his meannesses, I
shiver thru this his journal of winter '64, these
shallow self-messages, scribbled
garbled vanities, these
hoarded-up passages in vomited self-desire, naked,
entangled in falsities,
christened his gloom autonomous, frightened, secret, closed,
cloistered his song from her occult presages, & brooded aloof from her;
as Ginny, wondering, scried for him,
divined grim full diaries for sorrow,
or whispered of
seven profound orbits thru holiness allotted him/ & he mocked her.
foresaw more than he cd dream to/ & he feared her. dared
confounded her to contradiction; mocked her. dared
deride her to embitterments, & broke her. dared
enfold her & console her, in their darkness, where they cried.   o,
sothsegger, sothsegger scry, snow
gentleness from my sky on their wounding, wounded weird. & absolve them.

                    sung from a festering chasm here from now, un-
willing to be redeemed by losses / this late drift of ashes sweet my burnt sky down,
            wounding me with youth & nescience, how I
suffer my shy scarrd gristle upgroveling / erect divine Lion laughing & binding me,
            & implore to be force
            fed earth
            worms defild quit quick of
dying yes & has me as he has me strappt tight to my bed on my back his
            fingers upthrust harsh nails gouge has me
screaming muffled under my gag blasts rock up loud, clamps
            canines on my writhing & his belt repeatedly
& repeatedly as his young golden kneecaps sting my frozen gray
            hands, slops vodka past my gag, icecubes
stufft into my nostrils helpless pale thongbound wrists struggle glad, carolling
                                                                bloody.

                    120

revolution war bloody birth inside me trees crack cries in the night.
eroticized cynicism parcht godhead acacia whom the hot wind hurts.
I am not where I am, saith the mad Lord God.
where safest   lost my home,
& poetry upbraids me to these depths of my Godhead.
death simply to want safety, put a stop to it. more fire,
        pyre sweet,   raise me
wrench me wretched gasping red out of said unto thy song, Goddess,
        more fire,   pyre sweet,
who are the other people
wind in acacia
        sun doors hidden
                who are other people
                    four tangerine-colored carnations, two white
                        & rhythm-no-dancing & dancing-no-rhythm
                            burnisht-copper Irish setter wd rather not be petted
                                "I feel more of working in the blind" / pay
me back if you are able how will I smoke drive my car, eat. wind
in acacia. while the child's black puppy glassfed
   drags her dangling colon across my fresh spring grass, Goddess,
     more fire, pyre
        sweet, & lift me as loss & ashes thru my blue sun breath door.

yet not alive, never embraced alive, & his words, haunted,
indelible to recall it: stony, immobile, unflinching,
stubborn under his sudden yelled curses as he leaped at her,
out of his suffocated child uncontrollable, bursting, table up
ended radio exploded dinnerplates smasht lamps totaled
coffee cups splintered, blood-wet tomatoes burnt pork chops splattered, sliding
greasily down her scarified wall—& his chokt harsh fist, impotent, slasht,
gasht repeatedly against her shoulder, while
Ginny, my Ginny, neither cried out, nor stirred. & he fled,
orpheus of fraudulence prideblind under snowfall/ & she stared,
in her thralldom to her crystal where his phantom appeared,
singing their lone stark song, in vain. where-
ever in this his painstaking, resuffered, rhyme-enforct world,
faithful to the snowflake, solicitous of
ice, did he go wrong, huh; as merciless this rain
laments the bedarkened apartment of someone who feared
to touch & to dream & to sing from the gasping source, o
sothsegger, sothsegger scry, snow
astonishments from my sky on his feelingless weird/ & absolve me, absolve
absolve me.

wind in acacia.
elven wrinkled grinning, Greatgrandma Fair holds out her dead Irish arms to me.
I'm on my skates, Anacapa st. sidewalk, front of my aunt's house, in Santa Barbara.
      & I wd like to tell you what the sun felt then she felt cold.
I wd like to tell you what the moon felt like then he felt nothing & what can a song feel?
      spiders in the palmtrees. rattlers in the outhouse. something
      deep underneath the sidewalk when you put yr ear down. yeah.
poem, I drive without insurance for you I wash my socks for you I smoke to death.
mother dont die don't die I want to be near you as soon as I can, mother.
& poem, I am going to be to you what a man wd be to a man who wd love him: I swear.
      composed from a compost here from below,
grudgesgrunts-angstoinks-baby-creaming-on-anguish-stupord-&-
      muscled-Lion-snarling-&-mauling-me song: hungry to
      cry I'll keep quiet sir I'll keep
quiet sir but shrink me into my zeroing music of puncht-out rhythms of
      white knuckles pummeling, chest, lips, pummeld, singing
I can keep quiet sir I can keep quiet sir, & passing out, & coming to to
      no cant let him cant
      do this, stop, stop me, avid for, enthralld by
big boot death grum fugue death, dry fountain to wake to
to that memory of him crumpling my poems up, rasping thru my gag to try to to
      cry out but passing out, to wake to
to his lunatic stare above me sweat pouring down, my stomach knee-gougd, his fists
      battering my breasts, & endless my smile, & ecstatic my
fall, passing out, for how long now, coming to, in silence, to no one, in
      pain, ribs fracturd lodgd against lungs,
& to narrow this joy thru this glittering zero, to meet my vain first self
      abandond deserted one hand still tied,
 my poems everywhere scatterd, throat bruised, hammerd-in
song shut, halfway downstairs stumbling, panting wild to holler out my
      front door wide open on the great confusion, must
've dragged me into the bathroom, weakened & begging for sleep, floor splosht, walls
splosht, vomit, diarrhea, sickening ambers, eyes steely true shockt blue in
      mirrord face crazd hot, bloody but not
my face, not mine, or was it, or is it, teeth lips tongue glorying in Lion-tang
      & relishing my angerd-for, ineluctable, down, come.
      spiders in the palmtrees. rattlers in the outhouse. something
      deep underneath the sidewalk when you put yr ear down. yeah.

rhythms over rhythms on dim pre-
uterine foundation this stark
marsh path alongside unbreathe-
ing inlet waterweeds stricken, snappt under boot

thud, forest-cliff looming tall on our right, thick, o-
paque, blotting out sky
of the fishscal'd cloudscape, hiding
only dank blur glimmers of the furtive I
halt; Hank heads, bold, for the trees & I follow; halt, & final sun-
splotches off his umber suede shoulders striding squar'd into dread & I
follow, slow, on no clear old path to go by, no
sound, no ravencry, noonday going pale, & song—
song shivers

so I enter my unearthly forest & invincible weird,
lung-fire in dominance, dread of the struggle,
struggle in the song, on the side of song, against
my song, furtive blurs menace, wolves & bear uprear
in the corner of an eye o christ what made that cry
& how deep is this silence—memory—the way is
a memory, Hank are you sure of the way
back & I let myself sink in aspen leaves shimmering
pine needles crusht underfoot, I sink
into the dread forms, lung-fire scorching them,
& Hank, let's go back now, Hank, let's go back

for within this forest lies
my gasping son in a wreck in my sky & he dies & my dead
dad touches him, I cry out, I breathe again & this, this the satanic
black-bearded visage accusing from child-dream
rising from humus, & the stern god's ruddy thick phallus
plunges into my brain, implanting these rhythms I
wake in a chokt sweat, & who is she in a white thin gown who killd
the gold-strippt devourer of my clawd bloody shoulders,
who guides me to this moaning shore,
six shriveled females sit rocking in foam & in horror I
fall, kicking in a tantrum of dust on my holy
road, all creatures cornered die screeching NO
& my six deadly wives, bodies of wither'd stone,
long wet silver hair sheathing them,
squatting stupidly in the waves, mute, stoic, eternal,
weaving, as the waves submerge, reveal, submerge them, weaving,
shiny vessels of seaweed in the monotonous tide, their eyes
long gone empty in the brine, & the seaweed, dripping, flickers,
glistens burnt-amber thru their sacred
toiling/ Hank, let's go back now. Hank, let's go back

123

incessant disintegrations of music muscle my days jerked
        off solitary without second so
many vain messengers taking me for a dog I am a strippt dog
        child-cry dogshit this song or
songfraction for that snarld song Leland at 26 in 61 under
        tiresian narcissist fondling his firm
rich sunlit future above me stealing mine I let him glutton my lifesong
        my child hood in cold wild narrowing
gaze my malefic numinous ill process resigned to submitted to at
        last as deep as to infant-odd
first shitty seed brain's template or prime fault line my
        strong song's grum starter incessant dis
        integrations of music muscle,
& my days go dirtied; ways I slay my sweet blue temple / weird, weird
beauty, silence, nothing, erupting all these craving years to
        come on chest on cock on
stomach ankles knees clinging to my hair my face ecstatic down-
        rush hate-stifled vision-drag
kids in the vast diamond of gridset barracks joke dread half-hidden avoidance of
certain suddenloved men in streets or on coffeebreaks numinous ill void seeps
        into this rasa for that
        flawd song Leland,
strippt astounded exalted abased

o   & crablike out of navel brung unto dad crab
lice son snuck off to yr queers again? & pours
acrid brown lark
spur on my balls, dis-
gusted plucks at my armpits sideburns eyebrows ass w/my mom's
voice at the door last damn straw damn last damn straw & at dawn
this salt-fog hides my house where's my
mom, gone, son, gone, for
good & curses his wall as I cling to their fog-
lit doorknob, their pillows flung to their cold
floor, their sweatwrencht sheets clamming to his thighs as he
smokes, coughs, stubs burns small &
soft grey ashes fall on his white bare toes, dis-
gusted I watch him curl in his head & breathe in slow we swirl
quiet & alone under thick low fog swirl   o

& the dead raven we come upon, on the forest
                floor. sleek once to cleave
                        the boreal
air. twisted neck bent back over wing, great wings
                outspread in great
                        struggle. shines
decaying. ebony beak bloodspeckt,
                wrencht toward sky & eyes
                silver'd. underbelly of
                        maggots, ants
thru crawfeathers stirr'd by the low
                breeze. something
dead. gleaming like an onyx thru the shadowy
                forest

You hear? Sonny hush. from groin to
ground. Sonny that's all. one small
sobbing. arntcha glad? mother fall away.
I laugh all night,
slitherers in my skin. sing to my new
wrist-hairs. breastbone thrums.
thin ribs ring. those long-ago
dust-swirls. dream of a boarded-up
stairway.

my farm. sleep he
sighs. toadstools sprout from grandpa's chest.
    why are we here?
locks his withering arms sixtyfive years about me.
    he never did.
I feel his puckered thighstump on my thigh I
    never did I
do. always. stubs his chin against my throat.
    whose whispers ache.
that is whose whiskers. gray. wonder can I touch, shakes his
    head, eyes that cold
black book he ponders. mutters hell & damn. & true.
    ornery stare
blue thru tangled eyebrow bristles long & thick.
    our kerosene
lantern flickers. winged bugs drown. Grandpa Hickman,
    why are we here?
from groin to ground the language gripes in us.
    Sonny that's all.
instead sighs: sleep. git. I go I cry in bed I dream
    of the ocean
flooding my farm, look my grandpa's artificial leg
    & shiny shoe
float him thru woodlot. whose briny hands seek
    me I sink down.
you can't save me. don't want to be here with you,
    my cow she hates
you, chickens hate you, just swisschard for supper I
    hate your mean God.
red anthills burst from grandpa's chest. let's play cards.
    he reads his book.

126

I shout out curses to dried-up beanfields, flying
    ants I shatter
intricate forts with my stick. die. die. my devil
    I pray to you.
in wornout overalls I kneel down I kneel down. help dad & mom sell our
    bakersfield shack
 & get here quick. my damn grandpa won't wear his
    hearing-aid I
can't talk to him. undresses under the covers I
    can't even see
where his leg's cut off. won't wear his false
    teeth we can't eat
meat & it's lonesome for miles. swats at hutches
    with his cane. that
 riles up rabbits. cusses out chickens. cow got
    mad she took off.
dragged him clean over hayfield I helped him get up
    then he beat her.
& he won't play cards. my devil make mom & dad hurry.
    make grandpa scat.
night: thunderclouds crush thru grandpa's chest my farm
    churns into voice.
hopeless chickens griefstruck cow   one small sobbing
    bitter rabbits
weep in the choking throat   so my sleep opens:
    grandpa's crying.
daytimes I won't wander. I'll keep nearby. I'll
    fetch his hoe. come
dusk & I'll bring our cow in. hours at a stretch, oh
    he can read here.
in silence in his frontporch chair. look there go five
    P-38's.
miles beyond brittle limabeans in sun haze. this rain
    hits soft at first.
then thuds down hard. grandpa watches. mom said
    he'd studied once
to be a surgeon. why'd he stop? & dad left home,
    fifteen years old,
ran clear from Nebraska to ocean. we watch
    tall hollyhocks'
blooms break. fall. I bet I hear petals rip. rain
    stops. wet snailbacks

gleam. he licks his thumb. & he turns that page.
    fat fly-eggs slide
thru grandpa's chest. mom & dad get here at last.
    friday fish day.
mom fries fish. I poke my fork under skin.
    mom what's that? what's
what? ohmygawd look Lee there's maggots. Johnny,
    Cliff, stop eating.
grandpa, stop eating, there's maggots. he can't hear.
    he takes a bite.
GRANDPA THERE'S MAGGOTS. looks at his plate, glares
    at us. goes on
eating. GRANDPA THERE'S MAGGOTS. he goes on eating.
    mom clears our plates.
dad clears his throat, sucks in air. GRANDPA,
    DON'T EAT THAT. they're
cooked, ain't they? & he eats, glowering. mom starts to
    cry oh Lee I
just can't stand him anymore why can't your bakersfield
    sisters help out
some? they're his daughters. & my grandpa can't hear.
    that he's leaving.
from groin to ground the language gripes in us.
    we just got word.
Sonny he's dead. want to go with me?
    where? funeral.
no dad we weren't so close. stubs cigarette. stands.
    leans on kitchen
door & sucks in air. fists in pockets. sighs
    okeydoke, stares
at floorboards, then at me, one more sigh &
    okeydoke. now,
 spring weeds spring from grandpa's chest hello red
    chickens he's dead
arntcha glad? hello eucalyptus, hello limabeans,
    hello cow &
rabbits he's dead. hello swisschard in your shadowy
    bed the old man's
dead. my grandpa Orville Ray Hickman is
    dead. arntcha glad?

& Sonny my self my father my son how you are

choked in growth how strangling in saltbreath how hoisted to
cloudhood rainwrencht & angry as
you are   my farm lost will anybody give
dad a job or coasttown surfroar
treat my brain right & who talk to me tell me
where my head's going by night or day will mom
always gaze thru my screendoor dust to
puzzle buckled asphalt wherever it goes or out
kitchen windows at white
woodslat garagewall her diamond her golden
rings wet bright doubts in sinkboard doublelight?

I pound keys I smash into them listen to me listen my
      scuffed loafer on my loud pedal blasts
      elbows' rage knuckles' wrath
thru my cramped shoebox tonguetied stonedeaf house my dad
      slaps his paper shut yells shut that up-
      right right up so I slam my damn lid shut.
grandma on my own bunk in the wrong bedroom groans
o why can't you ever let a body nap?   & on my poor
      dunyellow frontporch mom's
cooing into the crib to slip a rubber nipple back
      between Nancy's pink lips & to tie
      a silver-ribboned bootie. there's Cliff,
asquat beside comicbooks on my sidewalk, John
      skinny & sweaty no teeshirt on
figure-eighting his bike on Chino Street. sun seeps
      glue thru my one parched tree. I can hear
laughter of mexicanguys from their end of my block
who don't like whitekids much & who play tough too
      rough anyway. hunched down
on my frontporch steps I glower. hum. stare
long into matted crabgrass until my eyes hit dirt.

& Sonny my self my father my son how you are
snatched up unknowing-knowing by padre pride his six
deadly wives their waves going green off & over
who drink saltwater who eat starfish who rise
undrowned out of surf   mouth thick with sea-
seeds to stuff down hungers hungers who keep
cold watch where hot eyes swim & how you are
boy-age, snared under, how

no ritual prohibitive will, can, take, how sorrowing
dad shall hunt me his lawknife grief-edged   howling of
shit & glaciers   over the dead rocks   under
my sea: *& they come for me the strong men who toss me*
high into sky as women & children shout get out get
out little boy go away little boy let mother go let
your mother fall away deep under but I have secrets carved
on my bare chest invisibly my intertwisted snakes of
poetry whose skins sprout anew & are new again & are wordskins
new & untouched & magic & shining & trembling & silent.

& I meet old Duane in Fox-Arlington dark his 50-
year-old knee pressed against mine his tobacco-brown
        fingers in my jeansfly that gold
eyetooth flashing   where can we meet kid I suck
his necco wafers his popcorn salty on my lips I say
        mom I'm going to the movies
        & pennies in my loafers   ribs
bare in breeze shirttails dangling jeans pulled low
        so hairs show I start shaking as
citybus squeals to a halt there's bald Duane in tan
        slacks orange socks red
sideburns, getting off, glancing sideways, scared.
        where do you live kid no Duane we
can't go to my house let's go up into those trees on
Mission Street oh crap kid we can't do it out-
        doors why not it's safe I
sprint across Chino in case mom's looking o jesus
        christ kid breathless but
        under pinetrees oaktrees
calm, staring while I strip   christ's sake boy
        why take all your clothes off
        & I'm stretching my sky against dry
needles & my dad throws the frontdoor open & the light falls
        sharp into my eyes I stop crying.

& Sonny my self my father my son how you are
safe under wordskins   *& the women surround me*
& they beat me with firesticks   & their breasts
& their eyelids   dripping sweat on me   & the men
carrying me binding me   on my back   in surf
whispering my ears full of nightmares   leaving me,

my burning firestick lifted high above foam.
& now my dark comes   & my six deadly wives
rise out of waves & become my waves & they lick me
my chest my knees my forehead my lips they
comfort me   & no one can cut my mother from me, no one
& I stab my firestick deep into wet I keep it mine
& out loud over surfroar I laugh all night at their night-
mares & my slitherers in my skin writhe joyous
& they sing to my new wrist-hairs   & they protect me
& I sink carved into sand & my mother's moon sinks   & I wait.

dad asks why I am crying I'm not crying, front-
  room light cuts front-
  porch dark   sun slices oak-
leaves   dappling my skin where Duane lies
  leans into me I
  stand   almost tall as
dad on my frontsteps mom heard you but dad I'm not
  crying he gazes
down at me my body these leaf shadows fluttering
chinstubble grazes my chin   my teeth clench   can't
  I go in dad my arms
  stiff at my sides on pine-
needles   sunflares   lick eyelids I
  squint   thru red
  sideburns   twist
my face away   taste where his tongue went   he
  chuckles   dad sighs
okay Sonny go on indoors go say goodnight to your mother
& he leaps up   curses   kids on the hill a girl
  screaming   boys shout he
darts into bushes I grab clothes   no time for
  buttons I run   run   not like on
juniorhighschool greentanktop trackteam straining
  baton forward to next tensed
  hand, wind whizzling my strong
whitelegs' brand new hairiness, lungs aflame, headhair
abounce, jockstrap prickledamp—but scared, barefoot,
  shirttails flying,
whimpering, jesus don't let them follow me, jesus
don't let them see where I live & behind hedge
  slipping shoes on, buttoning up—

        sprinting corner onto Chino
Street, leaping frontsteps easy closing screendoor slow
    hold my breath   look calm.

        & the men whisper I dreamed her. yes but I cry no.
        no dad please don't happen to me yet not yet not
        yet dad please don't happen to me. & my snakes
        quiver deep in my chest where their breath stops.
    & the men whisper she's not here she's never been here she's
    dead. & she died at my birth & she dies last night & she dies
        way before I was born & they whisper I dreamed her.

            & my snakes,
            wake up so hungry   ●

& I skid on my bike thru oak parks
sun hot on my gold cords,
    I stare / I stare.
wrinkled knuckles on gnarled laps
in noon-dusty cars I speed past,
    circle back, coast by,
        damp zippergap gaze / I stare.

    I stare on my stomach under palmtrees an old guy
just getting in his fordcar just freezes & sunlight
sucks tight at my swimtrunks so I roll fast over & split
    burnt knees wide, thrust my hips up

    & then he looks at me / & then he looks at me.

& then it opens as in a dream
    Santa Barbara Public Library
        basement mensroom swingdoor
my step narrow
wooden stairway downward
    & those long-ago dust-swirls
        begin again to rise.

around my torn sneakers, cuff-sand, silky
    see-thru new teeshirt,
skyblue my bellybutton navy my tits & LH
    inkblockt on my golden knees,

my corduroys pulled real low.
at bottom I can't find a door,
   I turn around jump it's
   here right in back of me,
at this dirtywood door to go thru & let
                        swallow me & it

      swings shut:

crumpled papertowels waterpools butts a leaky faucet.
   grayblue marblewall juts doorleft,
   hiding urinals from toilet stalls.
chickenwired frost-glass doors I can see thru.
   piss-smell out of every seam of
   redtile on floor whitetile on walls.
got a great hard-on, enter
   tiny dim cubicle two
   still gray urinals one inch too
high, stories & pictures, take out my
   hard-on, stoop to read, my
jaw slung, & a smell much lower, stronger, next to
chipped porcelain lips where grownups write kneeling,
   where choked ceiling-light in
   dustclogged cage
              won't sing.

                        & look,
my streaked shiny sink trembling old hands get so
   scrubbed up at,
& look, my stuck yellowgreen liquid soap dispenser,
   my way-high-up mirror, blue firing back
      thru sweaty hornrims,
      my breastbone thrums
      my thin ribs ring I
scowl on tiptoe I kiss me I lick me—

  & my snakes,
   wake up so hungry.
I stand over fire the smoke
stings into my eyes it wasn't
my real mother my real mother never dies.

I close my eyes,
my cockblood drips thru the flames   ●

       Saturdays after school sit slip
       bluejeans to loafers tuck up sailorshirt
       chest-high grownup messages scratcht
       in my wall I come down all the way from
       Gaviota where's the action in this
       town I was here where were you
       cockballs hung below kneecaps, eight
       inches make date & some days,
       toilets gone berserk, sick waters
       lurk on my tiles, sinkrust glistens
       faucet drips cobwebs wait I wait o
       only wrinkled eyes sneak over me o
       frost-glass door o & only dying
       men's shoes squeak me signals

       under my blue marble wall.
                        rest,
       headache on fists elbows on knees
                            go
           hungry go hungry go hungry.

           & one day
               I meet George
           & I watch
               as he combs his
           gray hair
               in my mensroom
           mirror
               & he asks me
           how old I am
               soon I'll be
           13
               & soon he
           lowers my
               levis down
           & soon he
               unbuttons my
           shirt too
               & presses

                his hands
                        on my shoulders
                could I
                        race
                my bike
                        slow
                thru the ocean

                        I can't
                swallow I
                        twist my
                head away
                        the white-stuff
                hits my
                        school-
                books
                        I stand up

                & his hands
                        on the small
                of my back
                        & I lean
                my forehead
                        on his tie

                & I whisper
                        the only time I
                ever did it
                        was with my best friend
                Jerry I
                        was 7 he
                combs his
                        gray hair
                in my
                        mirror

& one day says meet me upstairs.
hurry button levis hurry hurry. hard
sunlight. George, tense against stacks. kid, kid,
keep out of it. don't come around here.
        they watch this place.
don't let old men touch you, it will hurt you.

now, I don't know you.
　　　you don't know me—
yes I do, you're in that play at the Lobero,
I saw your picture in the News-Press.
you're George, & I whisper his last name.
hugs his briefcase to his chest. promise me
you won't tell. come downstairs with me George
then I won't. stay away from me kid.
don't go George, I won't tell, don't go!

& the men tie my wrists to the pole.
they show me their white wombscars.
they rip their wombscars open.
they lie, we are your mother, they lie.
& my father's knife cuts swiftly.
I beat my body back against wood.

& my father my father forces
blood past my lips my tongue

I move toward a mother not
theirs, my light in my song not

his, I spit out their blood I
hurl my embery firestick far

far high over surf, surf roars it
　　　out, the men shout
　　　when will you kill him

o when will you kill him so harsh my father
　　　groans to his knees & cries
& he cries to my ground my mother he kisses
the soft kiss of sorrow I sleep so

bound in a grave in his brain he leaves me alone, alone　　●

I won't be here for four Saturdays George
　　I have to make
my Confirmation at Our Lady of Sorrows I
I don't want more sins to confess to. he winks &
levis-on-argyles-hobbled I watch him go.
& he goes up in the flames that sever us.

136

my swingdoor closes he's gone.
those long-ago dust-swirls
gently
descend as in a dream

of a boarded-up stairway.
shirt still unbuttoned, levis still
at ankles,
in the mirror

my face wings hills & alone in my sky & my eyes hum
incomprehensible. this song
goes on & goes on
like this, dumb bright

to the end,
before we are forced crazed haters
in the all-hugging hate
we must hate

& before my snakes
are also wrencht
separate—my broken female
seeking down dark within me

her own far place to die,
& my honest male,
left grieving, left grieving, left
grieving.

Yellowknife Bay

under clouded noonsky, crossgraind, dry thunders muffled, whimper
of wind, last hours, Fort Providence, & hours-late bus, we wait
by hudson bay company, wooden porch steps, Slave
Indian children stare, frown, sullen-eyed; we board
mudcaked outback rattletrap, curses spat, dirtclods, rocks
flung after us; backfiring toward Yellowknife, Aussie
driver, Indian woman, two young Slave Indian men, Hank, me;
downpour again & overcast always; night; each riding silent, alone, & wind
whistling thru windowcracks; graveld highway, pitted;
swerve, slide, wheelslip; cold; impossible sleep;
lightning-lit poverties of villages, ancient tribes in their modern
                squalor; word-road, pitchdark;
wilderness unanswering; no signs for me; my forest un-
                yielding; word-rain, plainsong, pitchdark.

o   then as tho strangling, retting
each day more taciturn, dad
after she left him, the one
decade left him, trappt, in far worse sours than child stuff, roots
determining, so that even as he had at 15, his, dad, I had at 16 also
left him, as even
his angers left him, leaving
some tenderness &, as he told me,
an ache for one only he narrowed his heat to, held to,
put it in the work, son, put it in the work,
& a day came, all of his sons having left him,
& his daughter much more her mother's,
that I saw him standing still in that crowd of dead children, staring
heavy into the low flame of himself, & alone, like a stranger   o

unguided ungratified unillumined unslept
untoucht stunted passions debauch brutish down to daybreak
anywhere anyone   quick men   dead men   my nameless
city park dirt path spring lust fog
agitating largo out of Ferndell/ how I
        grasp myself priest in grum hickmaning dawn
self-addicted grave groyne sweat, this
habit fatidic withal, mine ascetic my listless slug;
mine inburied ephemeral upanishad moon,

extinguisht, inflames it, delights it; how ungrowing I gasp
uphill toward blackwillow, hidden, shadowed
reborn fresh morning spring creekside bird-
sung proud paleblossomd owl-home wingd-ant-home snake-home, song-home, my
        kiss-the-ground sanctum blackwillow;
reach hilltop, stop,
breathe in in sharp hurt in clear sudden sight of it, crisp
piercing first light thru tentative fog lift,
early leaf cry, soft seed shimmer, moving, breathing, swaying
unto itself alone how no one shd deceive it,
shaking, yet no breeze to disturb it;
       & I wonder, & I see:
giant, muscled, hardond, strippt
lunatic, writhing against treetrunk,
fragile seeds adrift in strange griefs around him,
fingertips on nipples, eyes half-closed, groaning,
watching my approach, not shifting his gaze away,
       dionysian long dark hair bejeweled yellowgreen,
young blackwillow leaves ensnard there, yellow blackwillow flowers fallen;
then in seedstorm under branches
shivering in my willowshell, spell-
bound, stunnd, how
wordless he sings to me, beckons to me, slave to his story, fierce
half-smile, shoulders, chest,
loins sweating pollenkisst/ his white torso,
harsh-breatht, archt against willow, his
thick thighs spread wide   & between them:
slender, living, stiff, low blackwillowlimb plungd-in upgouging,
       greast, abandond-to, ridden,
slid savaging grinding, crazd mean tight on,
thrashes his body back against dread, angrier, wilder,
& by his uprooted, panickt, uneartht outcry,
       begets this song,
anointed under showers of willowseed shaken downtrembling upon us.

o   nine two twelve. twelve four sixty. dad per-
haps wakes, his woman asleep, her grandson asleep, his head
aches, rises, dizzy, kitchen, lightswitch, coffee his head
ache retch blur boy hall fall help crash cup hand crash
chair & falls & falls & falls fumes & eyelids not any
air monoxide flutter like that. fast. silence. or dad perhaps
bolts out of dream-shriek, temples exploding, & the

139

woman beside him dead, the boy in the hallway,
dead, dashes, kitchen ache chair stumble crash slips retch
hand doorknob fall, fall, immediate night, dawn, noon, twilight,
night, dawn, noon, ringings, knockings, young man hollers, anybody,
nine, two, twelve, home? twelve, four, sixty, anybody,
dawn, dusk, dark, home? in all that dark? in all that dark?   o

coward of not climbing to my song's peak his warm
          semen rolls over me his
          handsome head thrown back falls
forward eyelids shut bends at waist abdomen pumping huge clencht fists
clampt against last sweet thighs' throes blond locks shook over forehead each un
          conscious gesture or breath gasp
sickening, doesn't speak or glance my way slides back onto chair
          heartbeat shadow flutters
under damp chest-hairs his breath slows, dulled gaze studies my
ceiling stupidly mouth gapes arms hung slack knees flung wide his
          swollen wet cockhead
          limp against bellysweat
matted hairs curl shattered blue temple glances sleepily at wrist-
          watch, reaches to my floor for
crumpled-up socks, burning, unmoving, come hardening, I watch belt
          buckle buckled zipper lockt cuff
links snappt into place tie knotted blond hair combed at my mirror, stoops
          to hack loud once into an
ashtray grabs jacket flicks lamp off lifts door-latch, peers
          thru dim light, groans
softly as we hear languid dawn rain start falling, falling,
          steps into hallway numinous ill door
falls shut on me

o   for the entire process is benign, don't
bury me with you dad don't, on a hill top, view of
Pacific, placed coffin, & I descended to it, work on what has been
spoild, & knelt beside him, entire process benign, raised
my left arm one finger toward sky, rested my right on
his silence, go in to my Hidden, earth rose around me, process
benign, passing thru blue sun breath door, shut it on
panic, put it in work, feeling my syllables falling, solid,
heavy, earth covered my shoulders, breathed the dust, what
alone my lone this is, law I die under, burial of
verve & of uplifted arm, my finger stoppt moving, all

my poets, Hidden   & the entire, process, benign   o

this song or section of song for that soild song Leland
        dawn dregs un-
wiped-off semen drying on his skin lies quiet there yet, old
        hollywood rooming-house
waking under rain neons sputter mad against sunrise next-door cell
        alcoholic fat man coughs
brittle greatgrandmothers faint early chirps down my hall I
        listen to traffic rise on selma, night
vanishes under Beckett & Faulkner at 26 in 61
        hid song thru my
flawd door, wounded blue temple where
        child-cry stops, where
        solace to my
self my light grows numinous seven tectonics of
soul heft song-peak must be yes anyone sung child in my
        fire years gone years
to go must be yes anyone sung fierce at my door, lordly
        beauty above below
behind before to my right to my left beyond this song for that
husht song Leland beginningless ignorance asleep in my
        brain as rain
        falls numinous ill
rasa falls still

on wet soil kneeling in my willowshell, near
broken giant breaking my husht seeds free, soon
to cease drifting over me   lost, ghost-human, kisses
earthkissing rhythm–tree, dresses, vanishes, fades from my story;
& my blackwillow song grown calm, solemn,
small birds, jays, bright blues, return,
my red ants up treetrunk, silver-wingd, flashing,
        how they signal my sunup;
sunbeams thru leaf-whispers onto low willowstub, glisten
of mucous, blood, sheer wings glint,
flying ants stumbling up phallus-staff, over
round-ridgd corona's blind eye, how
craftily he carvd it, despairing, exultant, defiant
        insane in his half-light;
now, blackwillow, blackwillow, hide me,
for I unbuckle memory, for I undo my name;

141

for I strip me to childhood;
        for I slide down onto you
fingertips on nipples, my thighs spread wide,
for you pierce me, ravage me, for you make me cry loud;
for I beat my body back against dread; for these poor songs' pounding;
for shook blossoms scatterd meaningless from yr sky;
for I sob, for I gibber, for I babble crude psalm;
        for I desecrate;
for I sing ashamed of my daylight.

o   o dad, look, I am buried here, with you
having grown or not grown as you dreamed me
got adventure & got ascared, dad, dad, my dad a
fugue that I rose like a ladder, outward of me,
I have wrongd every rung of, until
inward is stasis, no seizure
& song I wd hide in my light lies hidden
underground with me
song under song under song a
dissonance, with rhythm percussive, unflowing
& I can only whisper: song, song, song, how long are we buried here?   o

next day, Yellowknife New Town, mercenary, safe;
& bayward thru Old Town, quaint, & Latham Island bridge, Hank
leading; toward smoldering windborne garbage-stench, steep
downhill road where Dogbills die, warriors once,
slaveowners once, in their weatherd-dun box-huts by the dump;
last summer, drove ridge-route, L.A. to childhood, East
Bakersfield 2534 Lake Street not one bleakness changd, blight
amid blight; Indians; other poor; crossgraind oilsmoke sky; trees
dead; new boxes without frontyards, built on old frontyards,
memoried childscape crumbling behind them; no sidewalks, nothing
                green; transfixt, pitchdark,
gazing; frontstoop roof, 2-x-4 proppt, on dad's mean shack, decrepit; look,
                look, outhouse prison of pitchdark,
still standing; & I'm afraid; & my mother's afraid; fears
to be seen outdoors torn blue bathrobe flapping; suddenly
crying; why; why is she crying; in rain I see her; dark-haird,
wearing a blue bathrobe, standing still on planks that cover mud,
the way to the outhouse, in the storm, holding her
hands to her face, screaming, screaming; or I'm home from my canal, barefoot,
she's dressed-up, spitcurls auburn on her forehead, stands

on Lake Street with her suitcase; where are you going mommy;
o, sonny, she says, o, sonny, why did you come home so soon,
wait in the house, wait for yr father, & I stare thru the window,
                    taximan, taximan, sky getting pitchdark;
now, Dogbills hammer-up stormwindows; under us,
volcanic outcroppings, glacier-groovd, Hank & I
stumble wind-deafend down boulders to Yellowknife Bay,
indigo pitchdark vast waterscape tempestuous in windsquall,
                    ice-stifled under snowfall soon;
breathstopping wingbeat terror-squawk raven-clash vicious above us,
                    beak-stab, blood-spray, feather-fall;
bleak plainsong sky over Great Slave Lake; unutterable omens
                    singing me home.

o   in emergence from dadspace gentle wd I move
in harmony with rain as she guides the roots,
shifting their hungers, softening impacted graveground
muscles of sleep inform my rising, urge me to surface
lips & tongue in word-rain uncover the upward, I am lifted
into spaces my rhythms open, the sun is made sensible
in attentiveness to change-scent I come from the ground on
I can hear the beach, I can smell the ocean,
& from earth into sky I emerge onto grass,
my eye delights, & my lungs laugh   o

On my Confirmation Sunday, dawn
blood run down thorn down greeny skin
home from my paper-route, starving
there's mom's chocolate cake, I cut a slice
doll's teeth glistening in   agonies of twisting Jesus
I take a bite   quick! spit it out!   mom mom wake up my
Confirmation's ruind she speeds to the Rectory
elbows & knees pure dust in a sunray a
sleepy young priest I lower ragged peejays I scrunch
burning nearing boiling   did you swallow any?
I dream of the ocean   yes father   did you mean to?
flooding my farm   no father   then why did you wake me?
mom the priest he's wrong
it was devil's-food   where can we meet kid   devil's-food
my nun clicks her cricket I kneel at your altar my head tilts
at my dirtyword door to go thru & let swallow me my
priest drops you soft on my tongue

& my loft organ thunders   & my high choir shout
I rise from my knees I walk down my aisle I go out
thru my blue sun breath door blind
word-raining song of
Sonny   my Self   my Father   my Son
& my Mother here-
after & of how we
hide me
so down dark into me
hide me
in my light
in my
song's need singing

not afraid
not afraid

cd shed rage
shd love come

ELEMENTS

Hay River

FOR HENRY URBANOSKY

    Husht
squalid like my dad in a grave in my brain, burial of
      verve, blind dumb deaf wet grovel dis-
tances clampt gag & my mindfold tight on me can't
breathe or die Hank & I all my scraggled song dumpt go
      batterd out of night toward Great Slave
Lake this bus rattles over gravel ruts flat long dirt
forest road north one dark & a thin dark day under far-
      off lightning & gray nervous
boreal rainfall my writhen corpse who is me before me
      moans o for me o for me o to destroy me

& once my son dying

once my son dying late prayer dream I'm 9 years old in our old
      black jalopy   my dad
dead, dead in the front-seat in a black
      overcoat   my mom
      invisible   drives us
to my movies in my night-
time not on any road but high up, out
      in my sky where meteors
      shine thru her I lean
forward   between them my baby my son his gaze his gaze
      sunk in time in my night-
time daddy daddy he's dying my dad wakes up to
touch the tip of a finger to my baby's
chest I whimper I wail out loud my december
      gusts sing thru
      busted out windows my tattered up-
holstery flaps crazy in wind
                stream my teeth
chattery hey what theayter we goin at what movie what
      movie we gunnasee once we git there see the glow
      from my laughy live son late prayer dream
light my frozen dashboard my whole jalopy fiery how we blaze clear, clear
    out here in my wilderness   onward   onward

147

wilderness onward onward I'd die to
        go into that forest & never come out what did
        you say Hank says I say I
said I'd die to hide in this forest/I see her in a sudden
drizzly clearing   visions you ache for & ache you, they
gnaw rake wrench split you & carve you in they gnaw, stock-
        still, torn skirt bleak sweater boots &
gusty about her in mazy twilight her dying eyelids lift
        toward the downrush glide
        of the solitary
raven swooping deep into wet glittery aspen shadows she holds
armload of dampt kindling whitehaired Slave Indian crone & children
        run past her into the hut with kindling
& the rain, whispery upon her somber face she burns
rigid toward gray over ancient glade my bus roars by I
twist in my seat to see her buried under branches how they
        thicken between us & cover her
        how I cover her here in my interior
grave her gaze motionless toward gray her raven winging within me
        thru rain spray chill in last
pure wonder & now: Hay River, Old Town, on this cold
        southern shore

toward cold southern shore, forest dusky
        trails muddy, icy
        scud, low sunrays slat I listen for
        source sound enfold guide me to my-
self, hide me in the, at first far-off frail
        moan in my spine, Hank
leads on running soon spruce & aspen thunder the
        rumbling en-
        gulfs me some-
thing beyond convulsive suffers seethes
        rages in itself, Hank
        bolts forward, breaks
        thru my final
        trees I am pulled, skulled
thru my wrench Woven-Here down stark hard sand Great Slave
        Lake's gnarled uprushing roar
shudders daemonic its groan thru me my night sun-
        light gleams blood-rust on my waves, gleams
off floating tree-hulks far out adrift sinking &

heaved huge black in
slow moiling cry wind squalls sand, leaves, over weatherbleacht tree-
    trunks washed up on
shore ragged roots flare gaunt against lightning I gaze I gaze
    long into my night how lost my light goes

The Hidden

FOR HARRY E. NORTHUP

o   law I die
under nothing to do with free
kind my brutish
law. out
law miracle, crawl, sweat, to glory, got
adventure & got ascared, dad, dad, my dad, a
version, blue eyes under silt by sea not light not light not
work on what has been spoild nor furthers
my work on what has been spoild   o

o   all the poets are Hidden. stoned
occlusion bursts into word-rain, dad songs
me high thru my blue sun breath door I cry I
cry war my jews my japs die, dad at canal red shoulder white
thigh, hate
him, tell, tell, re-tell, how the time's
hard, oat slabs
float in the lard, dad, grit in the kids' swiss
chard, stink bugs
fart in the yard   o

o   to nothing, no not
to nothing to
this this is this, what
alone my lone this is, great beyond
lazy wild sky in my fingertip, right ring
buried bunkbed splinter dad gouges my blood of nightly, for
me, & licks for me speechless, dis-
figured flesh-sign worried with a needle o, how many sun
downs dad got us down we awestruck divine we go to? I sing
this yr one poor gift for lack of one better my scar my gully
& way-gone 34 orbits later, tell   re-tell   o

o   this is no
saxophone solo dad but I can sing I can make it
all, yr frycook cuss wingspan riveter teethsuck flat times flat
broke ball-peen clawhammer crosscut bevel, level,
plane, make it all & yr odd sharp stare past me thru

lost Bakersfield Calif shack sunbeam dust,
past forsook Nebraska farther back alone dad I can make it all
well, with my tremolo learnt in school sweet & high
to yr sapphire birthstone beltbuckle knuckles long blond eye
lashes clear up there on a peace   ful sum   mers eve   ning when
the sun   HAS   set don't bury me with you dad don't
bury me with you don't   o

o   & jagged from Lockheed   & bitter   hisses
belt out of belt loops   lashes ass often   how I
must cringe   hate   breathe in in
secret   grow nervous ecstatic Hidden   set fire
to ladybugs   weep   hurt fat girls   weep   seek boys to
scorn me   dig in my dark my shovel snaps breast
bones   & how out loud wd I shout it   shout it out
fierce   whip me dad whip me whip me til he crumples   & caves
in   in me   whimpers Sonny   scat far you go task what lights
of yr catechisms   whip you   task barren
trees   barren skies   whip you   task any
sad   wrong   old   road   beat you & wail
all yr poets Hidden son I nail my breath door tight & still   o

o   one blond slim 1949 dad's one solid stunnd
noonburnd carpenter on his own poor man's plumbd
redwood rooftop beveld & groind against one gruff song
from our longwinded sky in a glare under far blue sun
who stonefaced stares down at a boy
skinny & scribbling at the wheel of the stalld black jalopy those harsh
hardond mystical clear
groans got forgotten whose unclear
glance flashes breathtaken high
into his breathtaking higher up enemy's eye & both do remember
that ocean in their brains where it rains forever. only as long
as one quick flare wch fire flings slick down his naked spine
that the man wrenches back to hammer & shinglestack,
& the boy in the black wreck falls back to his fresh black song   o

o   & crablike out of navel brung unto dad crab
lice son snuck off to yr queers again? & pours
acrid brown lark
spur on my balls, dis-
gusted plucks at my armpits sideburns eyebrows ass w/mom's

voice at the door last damn straw damn last damn straw & at dawn
this salt-fog hides my house where's my
mom, gone, son, gone, for
good & curses his wall as I cling to their fog-
lit doorknob, their pillows flung to their cold
floor, their sweatwrencht sheets clamming to his thighs as he
smokes, coughs, stubs burns small &
soft grey ashes fall on his white bare toes, dis-
gusted I watch him curl in his head & breathe in slow we swirl
quiet & alone under thick low fog swirl   o

o   then as tho strangling, retting
each day more taciturn, dad
after she left him, the one
decade left him, trappt, in far worse sours than child stuff, roots
determining, so that even as he had at 15, his, dad, I had at 16 also
left him, as even
his angers left him, leaving
some tenderness &, as he told me,
an ache for one only he narrowed his heat to, held to,
put it in the work, son, put it in the work,
& a day came, all of his sons having left him,
& his daughter much more her mother's,
that I saw him standing still in that crowd of dead children, staring
heavy into the low flame of himself, & alone, like a stranger   o

o   nine two twelve. twelve four sixty. dad per-
haps wakes, his woman asleep, her grandson asleep, his head
aches, rises, dizzy, kitchen, lightswitch, coffee his head
ache retch blur boy hall fall help crash cup hand crash
chair & falls & falls & falls fumes & eyelids not any
air monoxide flutter like that. fast. silence. or dad perhaps
bolts out of dream-shriek, temples exploding, & the
woman beside him dead, the boy in the hallway,
dead, dashes, kitchen ache chair stumble crash slips retch
hand doorknob fall, fall, immediate night, dawn, noon, twilight,
night, dawn, noon, ringings, knockings, young man hollers, anybody,
nine, two, twelve, home? twelve, four, sixty, anybody,
dawn, dusk, dark, home? in all that dark? in all that dark?   o

o   for the entire process is benign, don't
bury me with you dad don't, on a hill top, view of

Pacific, placed coffin, & I descended to it, work on what has been
spoild, & knelt beside him, entire process benign, raised
my left arm one finger toward sky, rested my right on
his silence, go in to my Hidden, earth rose around me, process
benign, passing thru blue sun breath door, shut it on
panic, put it in work, feeling my syllables falling, solid,
heavy, earth covered my shoulders, breathed the dust, what
alone my lone this is, law I die under, burial of
verve & of uplifted arm, my finger stoppt moving, all
my poets, Hidden   & the entire, process, benign   o

o   o dad, look, I am buried here, with you
having grown or not grown as you dreamed me
got adventure & got ascared, dad, dad, my dad a
fugue that I rose like a ladder, outward of me,
I have wrongd every rung of, until
inward is stasis, no seizure
& song I wd hide in my light lies hidden
underground with me
song under song under song a
dissonance, with rhythm percussive, unflowing
& I can only whisper: song, song, song, how long are we buried here?   o

o   in emergence from dadspace gentle wd I move
in harmony with rain as she guides the roots,
shifting their hungers, softening impacted graveground
muscles of sleep inform my rising, urge me to surface
lips & tongue in word-rain uncover the upward, I am lifted
into spaces my rhythms open, the sun is made sensible
in attentiveness to change-scent I come from the ground on
I can hear the beach, I can smell the ocean,
& from earth into sky I emerge onto grass,
my eye delights, & my lungs laugh   o

O Blue Temple

FOR WILLIAM MOHR

this song or segment of song for that flawd song Leland at
       26 in 61 tongue out dripping for
       balm in the corrupt
land bereft angry hungry weeping
male snake of that time in my dark those pale hard headlights wove
       over my dusty ceiling from
cars beneath my window, wide open on selma my
       gay young hustlers
lust bereft angry hungry weeping where
Beckett Faulkner at a loss glare down that my
       strong song's urge
       hoist me higher in my malign
fire this song or fragment of song for that snarld song Leland at
       26 in 61 isolate rubble down gutters shuffler in
our thick spit pool of absolute freedoms against the law to be
       legal, heritage bilge trash, out still for
balm in glutton land policemen to kneel to to pray to, mostly a
       lone in Los Angeles aching
all down selma vine to highland hardon bared icy in drizzle shouting
       four a.m. hank cinq at lung top get a guy
fuck me in azaleas spit on my face slap me by the church at las palmas
       way we slay the blue temple/ weird
wanderings of my subtle body

at 26 in 61 noon yet void seeps in yet noon my noon years
       solitary without second
nights I delve inward tensions remember breath cry deep joints un
       fold thru street mist from hunger here,
inchoate, male snake of the time, I, void rain-seep
       steep down arroyos steaming junctures my
seven tectonic plates of soul on bed edge in heat of
       hotplate in stink of crackt boots drying I
dream again under Beckett & Faulkner in flame-bait or rain-drunk
       rooming-house cell/selma at mccadden
place/parkinglot now next-door cell alcoholic fat man fright
       at dim hall's lost end two
       brittle greatgrandmothers fright
dying so quickly waking up slow to cold untold inside;

skinny guys with angry-cock acne, suckt off because lonely motor
          cyclists from corner hot
dog stand tight-butt young marines grimy in slept-in
          civvies I pose naked at my
window pulse grounded in headlight
glow drivers shivering hardup past incessant disintegrations of
          music muscle my years go,
          way I slay my blue temple/ weird, weird
waverings of my subtle body

song: rude poetics black levis white windbreaker way past last-call
          song: beginningless ignorance, sprung
          from american warlike childhood meek
under hollywood streetlights brakescreech searchlights cops or harsh
cold shoulders in shadow'd alleys subtle body sung low as I slide
          quick to my knees on glistening
pavement by wet thornbush, beginningless ignorance under my
          tongue my shut eyelids my
far-in young thunders growling tense smoking hunting atremble on
corners says no says no say yes yes yes, coward of not
          climbing to my song's peak way I
          slay my blue temple, neons
sputter mad against sunrise remember my phone number call me, call me;
          at 26 in 61 tiresian setup hidden
underlife flare-up sleek night-jag idling as grinned-at Leland gets
          in next to undreamt-of
proud blond messenger urgent demands disorder him abrupt to his
          eyes fierce beauty how it doth leap
Leland up rickety stairway selma at mccadden with his sudden one,
          beginningless ignorance how it doth lock
world-door after them Leland flicks lamp off they stand
          alone mute unknowing beginningless
ignorance how it doth scare

apprehensive rasa-risk open to numinous ill process or blue
          temple be wounded grum void seep in/
shapeshifter tectonics mnemonics beginningless ignorance high over snake
          bed I go back headlights streak ceiling at 26 in
61 tremble before him begin being child until I am all child, whisper my
          questions reach thru dark to touch on tiptoe to kiss
him whisper my questions, why he will not speak or move, why he
          shoves me away, turns to my

155

window street wet below says do what I want falls
        mute cold beginningless
ignorance waits, repeats, do what I want, I whisper, tell me, as cars
        shiver slow past numinous
        ill process his young
gruff words seep in where strength flails where doubt fucks temple down, wind-
breaker T-shirt boots black levis sweet naked for this guy my
        pale elbows dirty knees, dumb-
struck, shoulderblades helpless begun being child all child all
        child lie down on yr bunk I do I lie down;
uprush song temblor for this strippt song Leland as
fierce lordly beauty coming my way flicks lamp on, stay
        still stay quiet under breath under
        cold wild narrowing gaze be
ginningless ignorance how it doth quake me

everpassing autos hum wet over street below sacramental
        process slips jacket off I lie
        in subtle husht boy-thin
body beneath numinous ill gaze under lamplight, undoes
cufflinks, tie, I reach out to touch, no you can never touch me, doffs
        shirt shoes socks unbuckles belt-
buckle my cock up bright o hoist me higher in my harsh malign fire this
        ragged rasa for stern aloof beauty whose
tight black slacks inch low down slow over hard rock silence be
ginningless ignorance sprung music-muscle gleam-tippt at large & at
        lung-top crowing all
        child all child all child; o
where there used to be sky after dust; dad, mom, off to their warplant;
        I wd lie all alone in tall temples of grass in
midnights of other songs. must be anyone sung in my fire. years gone,
        years go. fierce
beauty, above, below, behind, before, to my right, to my left, beyond, must be
        anyone song my door. lordly
beauty mute unmoving my hands can neither reach him nor touch
        my own subtle
body (stay hurt stay isolate under numinous ill process, flawd
        song, strippt child-cry
astounded exalted abased / obey

incessant disintegrations of music muscle my days jerked
        off solitary without second so

many vain messengers taking me for a dog I am a strippt dog
        child-cry dogshit this song or
songfraction for that snarld song Leland at 26 in 61 under
        tiresian narcissist fondling his firm
rich sunlit future above me stealing mine I let him glutton my lifesong
        my childhood in cold wild narrowing
gaze my malefic numinous ill process resigned to submitted to at
        last as deep as to infant-odd
first shitty seed brain's template or prime fault line my
        strong song's grum starter incessant dis
        integrations of music muscle,
& my days go dirtied; ways I slay my sweet blue temple / weird, weird
beauty, silence, nothing, erupting all these craving years to
        come on chest on cock on
stomach ankles knees clinging to my hair my face ecstatic down-
        rush hate-stifled vision-drag
kids in the vast diamond of gridset barracks joke dread half-hidden avoidance of
certain suddenloved men in streets or on coffeebreaks numinous ill void seeps
        into this rasa for that
        flawd song Leland,
strippt astounded exalted abased

coward of not climbing to my song's peak his warm
        semen rolls over me his
        handsome head thrown back falls
forward eyelids shut bends at waist abdomen pumping huge clencht fists
clampt against last sweet thighs' throes blond locks shook over forehead each un
        conscious gesture or breath gasp
sickening, doesn't speak or glance my way slides back onto chair
        heartbeat shadow flutters
under damp chest-hairs his breath slows, dulled gaze studies my
ceiling stupidly mouth gapes arms hung slack knees flung wide his
        swollen wet cockhead
        limp against bellysweat
matted hairs curl shattered blue temple glances sleepily at wrist-
        watch, reaches to my floor for
crumpled-up socks, burning, unmoving, come hardening, I watch belt
        buckle buckled zipper lockt cuff
links snappt into place tie knotted blond hair combed at my mirror, stoops
        to hack loud once into an
ashtray grabs jacket flicks lamp off lifts door-latch, peers
        thru dim light, groans

157

softly as we hear languid dawn rain start falling, falling,
        steps into hallway numinous ill door
falls shut on me

this song or section of song for that soild song Leland
        dawn dregs un-
wiped-off semen drying on his skin lies quiet there yet, old
        hollywood rooming-house
waking under rain neons sputter mad against sunrise next-door cell
        alcoholic fat man coughs
brittle greatgrandmothers faint early chirps down my hall I
        listen to traffic rise on selma, night
vanishes under Beckett & Faulkner at 26 in 61
        hid song thru my
flawd door, wounded blue temple where
        child-cry stops, where
        solace to my
self my light grows numinous seven tectonics of
soul heft song-peak must be yes anyone sung child in my
        fire years gone years
to go must be yes anyone sung fierce at my door, lordly
        beauty above below
behind before to my right to my left beyond this song for that
husht song Leland beginningless ignorance asleep in my
        brain as rain
        falls numinous ill
rasa falls still

Picasso Deathday Night

FOR JOSEPH HANSEN

slow motion explosion lone grebe on the beach.
please don't kill me sir please don't kill me sir.
sick to my self hard work working inward.
(four colors azalean—don't forget it—distinct tart aftertastes.
      so then under what acid glare sequester my squalor-born
      deformed song body please sir don't
      kill me don't kill me sir please.
      w/just enough razor-slatch in levis crotch (now it's caught me/I cut
          wild left melrose blood surges turgid thru steel
          cockringd tight-thongd testes pufft-up high mass purple
          and early already danger-queen cruel   ripping
thru my shark skinnd night don't like shark skinnd but ripping, ripping

      manzanita manzanita sycamore locoweed creosote oak lone gray
         grebe grebe grebe grebe grebe grebe grebe grebe

running scared not much to fall back on throat dry to sing then
roots squirm upward roof of mother's ocean clutching song of
      terrified to tell you. how can I go on

rhythm-driven danger-queen M/B Club scurrying crotch to crotch, loud
      dope music amyl stink boys' tongues hands all parts of me, dimlit sweat
      narrow rooms boots crowds me kneeling surrounded eyebrows dripping
      salt. terrified to sing me. how can I go on

umbilical cord word-jerkt, eyelid cells meshing in darkness, this song
      hates me, wants me to breathe its breath away, he moves away,
      leather-jacketed, tall, who won't speak, I follow him, hot room to
      hot room, sidling-up, close to him, who won't even look my way, I
      beg him, this song, terrified, to grow, to be born, I beg him, he moves
      away, I follow, I whimper, I beg him

& my song is terrible for me this song burns a terrible no inside me whilst I write.
it cries out, not to have to dredge up hard-edgd cries, for me brutal, for me harsh, hates
      force, how can I force it, sing what I want, when I want, how can I go on,
      liar as craving it, liar as lusting for it, liar in the dark, see the needle,
      old man's cock, & see him pierce it, to see an old guy cry, & I beg him,
      do it to me too o do it to me too o please don't walk away o christ this song

won't ever be born, doesn't want to be born, & how can I go on

manzanita manzanita sycamore locoweed creosote oak lone gray
  grebe grebe grebe grebe grebe grebe grebe grebe

running scared not much to fall back on throat dry try to sing then
 gunning to climax on melrose, again on my old meat lookout my song snares
 no one no one on robertson sidestreets 4 a.m. strung-out on fair

fax erratic on santa monica chugging slow past corners boy hitch
  hikers fresh gashes fleshflashing take me take me nowhere no one no one
  in tradesman dark back-alley my lights out & on selma heads shaking no one no one on
  sunset; on vine, on vine, bedraggled, unshaven, one un

smiling one & my hands tremble breath races eyes glaze over you going far? not
  far I cut wild left from the right lane thru red light sudden siren
  shrieks I pull over fast o shit man he moans oh man fuck this here shit man
  ready to cry, we wait frozen thru the make on us, they drag him out,
  handcuff him, you want me to call anyone? no man no one head bowed ready to
  kill I gun off to song climax nowhere on no one & how can I go on

manzanita manzanita sycamore locoweed creosote oak lone gray
  grebe grebe grebe grebe grebe grebe grebe grebe

& my song is terrible for me this song churns a terrible no inside me whilst I write.
  speeding on hollywood boulevard furious before dawn tidal wave thrashing
  walls of mother's ocean when my head dies down I can feel it

then screech-halt last chance underage thumb-out gee thanks for the lift mister
  wrinklefaced scragglehaird hunchback shiverer in a lost workshirt
  scrawny pale-neckt fear-pitcht stutterer hyperactive eyebrows & hand-wrencher,
  so then I drive gentle, I croon slow, lovingly, until he nods yessir, okay sir
  & then shift into low cruel danger-queen quiet, frightening our misted hills

& where sycamore locoweed creosote sleep & liveoak guards owl & deer, here, take my hand
  whispering, stumble him up overgrown paths soakt weeds chin-high
  trap him in a shadow of branches when my head dies down will I feel it
  take me out of here, o god, let me go, you do what I want, yessir, okay sir
  when my head dies down can I heal it, hide his clothes on hillside
  stark white humpback trembling, tidal wave thrashing on shores of mother's
  ocean, what do you think you're doing sir o what are you doing sir

hunchback in my song under hard belt-blows, pleading, obeying all warnings,
    deformed song body, writhing, choking, gritting his teeth thru song-beat,
    please don't sing of me, please don't sing of me, on hands knees crawling,
    slipping, twisting thru brambled rhythms, stop, stop, what are you doing,
    dust made mud by dew streaking his body original terror in his hoarse
    young cry please don't kill me sir o please don't kill me sir & my
    whole wild hill shrills fire

I drop my belt, he stands there shaking, is it over? is it all over? wasn't it real?
    no, kid, playacting, joking, playacting, begins to cry & I hold him, this song
    hates me, wants me to stifle its life away, safe/unsafe his terrified way,
    doesn't want to be born or sing of me in dirt near azalea branches, sick to my
    self, hung-over, breaking, tearing, swallowing my bright pure petals & I
    wonder is it over, I curl up on earth under flowers, I wonder, is it all
    over?

      & pinkster & cardinal & salmon-rose & snow;
         & how can I go on;
    & curld 38-yr-old foetal position ear to my dry ground crying;
    & bitter azalean tiresian song;
         & how can I go on;

& morning squeezes forces me thru crevice unto glare so then I lift
    my deformd song body to my blue sun risen low
    over turbulent horizon slow motion explosion lone gray
    grebe grebe grebe grebe grebe grebe grebe grebe
& how can I go on;
    & pinkster & cardinal & salmon-rose & snow;
    & how can I go on

Fort Providence

FOR JAMES KRUSOE

& about how lost my light goes & about
cruelty my contemporary, about my way things are, about
my first eerie view of my lake hay river deserted september trembling,
tiresias sleepless raging from my malevolent lake, & about gross
cruelty to my song, my way thing are my contemporary, about these
climates strange fauna, what my line strains forward, giant
ravens motionless gaunt at my forest's black edge guarding
my oracular writhen lake under rain—small stark hope
from moribund hinterground wrenching my anger toward stabs of the
lightning, loveless grim roar my furious lake my sunset about
about what I have handcufft, about
what I have tortured, about
what I have severed the songs of I don't

dream anymore know where it's going great slave lake
sang me go down & go down, stand still in my thunder & hear it,
slasht tongues of vision scream far into dark. no death.
no death a strong dark a sun-trip a burning a sweeping, strict
pitch dark, all of it, & no death, no death, fire
flow, stars, quake hot, leaves of my nightmare, quiver!
I want to see all of it happen, I want my blue sun breath door wide open, I want
inevitable spreading joke & disease, white noise from my flute, gray soft
hairs of his damp perineum brusht against eyelids soundproof room rust-red
sand lake's edge at last ray flickering deep into my long tender blind
sinuous tremulous grasses no merciless ending tó it

& about how far off omega & about how much yet undetected
strangeness, scion of
naked charm, blue sun breath—symmetry's gasping child a river a calm
power listlessly overcast subarctic heavens restless, hesitant
rain my buried song drumming synaptic explosion flow no
merciless ending tó it & dying dying to continue ache-
ing, riverbarge now groaning my old bus over, & I here grippt on deck for
revelation downriver, tiresias river, striving oracular shapeshifting
rasa-river, huncht here tight against waterdrops, whipping in
wind long hair overcoat focust on risk what will be about bright
languages, bred of ravens rivertongues black galaxy'd gnats in my sun-
clash, & husht under fugue of the forest, where song—

song shivers

internal estrangement betrayal stern river convulse
me; no welcome from my sacred wildness, about
this childish swoon state I exalt into manic dismay this
frenzied seeking along my blue sun river
for the "poetics of this situation not yet figured out,"
I have to breathe one. about no power
to be heald thru my song
& what can I sing them, what can I bring them, build up my
work's queer fused rasa
love it hide it hate it uphold it, about
that old Slave Indian mending or caulking his boat by the river

a ministering cause to unlock the insoluble problems of the work
mending his boat by the river in my mind forever
& no glance nor any note of me taken
bald tiresian, early morning sun blinding off the water as I pass by, stifled.
& o which form direct action (what we sing about will affect you.
o which form direct action, this weedsrabid graveyard
for transgressors of wilderness, three bright ravens above me,
& no glance nor any note of me taken for that I am unclean I have
dared set foot in his stillness because I have none; none.
my wise fierce river exaggerated, depths of my formidable
tangle of aspens & pines in gusty september exaggerated, giant gleaming
ravens exaggerated, exaggerated   my pale thin skin
in the isolated, luminous place

internal estrangement betrayal stern river convulse
me, o teach, wrong how I have gone, where, when wrong, I go,
living vulcanian riverlight, erupt & cry in me loving, break, break,
deepest cleanest seed   rhythms visions firm my
freshskinnd unlockt prayer: two tall, dusky-skinnd
Slaves, severe glances sullen sidelong, unspeaking (I
flail at these gusts of gnats, or of spirits, or
of their green gold weir their familiars/ who
pass me on this dirt narrow trail from their own sweet
proud village, who as if in despite of despising me stride
to their childhoods' river & launch their trim canoe,
cross calm marsh arm, beach on the far beach, young, strong,
shirts open, sleeves uprolld in cold over
muscular understandings, who squatting smoke & stare at me & I

am wrencht by iron-black broad-stretcht wings grace thru my chaos gliding
one long, sure, even-held breath streaking low over the water
vanishing into the gold-leav'd mystery, Providence
Island, & my hurt song, whimpers, wd follow, follow, my single
raven, wrong, wrong how I have gone, & where, when wrong, I do go

rhythms over rhythms on dim pre-
uterine foundation this stark
marsh path alongside unbreathe-
ing inlet waterweeds stricken, snappt under boot
thud, forest-cliff looming tall on our right, thick, o-
paque, blotting out sky
of the fishscal'd cloudscape, hiding
only dank blur glimmers of the furtive I
halt; Hank heads, bold, for the trees & I follow; halt, & final sun-
splotches off his umber suede shoulders striding squar'd into dread & I
follow, slow, on no clear old path to go by, no
sound, no ravencry, noonday going pale, & song—
song shivers

so I enter my unearthly forest & invincible weird,
lung-fire in dominance, dread of the struggle,
struggle in the song, on the side of song, against
my song, furtive blurs menace, wolves & bear uprear
in the corner of an eye o christ what made that cry
& how deep is this silence—memory—the way is
a memory, Hank are you sure of the way
back & I let myself sink in aspen leaves shimmering,
pine needles crusht underfoot, I sink
into the dread forms, lung-fire scorching them,
& Hank, let's go back now, Hank, let's go back

for within this forest lies
my gasping son in a wreck in my sky & he dies & my dead
dad touches him, I cry out, I breathe again & this, this the satanic
black-bearded visage accusing from child-dream
rising from humus, & the stern god's ruddy thick phallus
plunges into my brain, implanting these rhythms I
wake in a chokt sweat, & who is she in a white thin gown who killd
the gold-strippt devourer of my clawd bloody shoulders,
who guides me to this moaning shore,
six shriveled females sit rocking in foam & in horror I

fall, kicking in a tantrum of dust on my holy
road, all creatures cornered die screeching NO
& my six deadly wives, bodies of wither'd stone,
long wet silver hair sheathing them,
squatting stupidly in the waves, mute, stoic, eternal,
weaving, as the waves submerge, reveal, submerge them, weaving,
shiny vessels of seaweed in the monotonous tide, their eyes
long gone empty in the brine, & the seaweed, dripping, flickers,
glistens burnt-amber thru their sacred
toiling/ Hank, let's go back now. Hank, let's go back

& the dead raven we come upon, on the forest
          floor, sleek once to cleave
                    the boreal
air. twisted neck bent back over wing, great wings
          outspread in great
                    struggle, shines
decaying. ebony beak bloodspeckt,
          wrencht toward sky & eyes
          silver'd. underbelly of
                    maggots, ants
thru crawfeathers stirr'd by the low
          breeze. something
dead. gleaming like an onyx thru the shadowy
          forest

Aphroditos Phalanthos

FOR DEENA METZGER

& then into dung to be heavend I was ever thralld, & to plunge my
         swollen voice
thru this black hole inside me wherein each song
's compacted made dense melodious my last
         song my first I alone
sing, hello now let me tempt stranger I need I need, come
         quick & he does come, he does
                  come
                      young
                            so strong
                                    wrenching
         my world's wet innocence out
of his body all wrappt in bronze muscle he is music he is singing:

         how well it is I am not afraid. & how well I am
         not afraid, not afraid. & how well it is I am not afraid.

now, show me my blue-lippt children stilld & curld on the stone teat.

         not afraid.   & he is music.   not afraid.

                  cd shed rage
                  shd love come.

however he come:
         in suntanned form of whore with navyblue flight bag
         fills, takes, orders, wearing sneakers or barefoot
         kisses hugs suckles, believable with the bullwhip, reasonable
         rates, dope not included, or

in moonlit widow's form, Jeanne, hesitant, delicate under the black
         nightfall cascading down her shoulders & her back,

         unafraid.   & she is music. unafraid.

                  cd shed rage
                  shd love come.

166

now, show me my embarrassing ones my despised ones my troubled ones.
        I've come to burst the death skin off you.

o, hopeful & attentive sentences: forever. sunshine acid penetrates
        nerves, upflutters those amorous high
        emberd leaves amberd clouds out there, where my
        shrieking kindless blvd weaves, & I spy him:

crossing calm against traffic to command this tremulous this exultant door/ worried
        uncertain
        narcissistic nostrils, eyebrows, serious
        eyes/ much more

than ever I have hope for: man, man,
        shivering & afraid at cold summer's cold eyes. older these
        hungrier fantasies unsnarld & writhe
        on the floor, at yr feet, where you stare,

on earth, with form & with affliction.
or, Jeanne sing my newborn song in New York to the spring skies, then!

for then! one spring & a summer, sweet widow Jeanne my muse/ or now
        was his name Brian? grins, steps clean of his clothes—

When you have been fuckt by so many hundreds of darknesses
So many summery fusions over the crumbled sill, receiver of
Stolen goods a key to the brain's room
                                o little piggy-piggy,
You run for the high devastations fires pursue & the harsh wind
favors. & not getting it sung. not getting it sung. she was
here during the early songs with her black silken hair she
                                greeted them smiling,
tentative understandings & solemn, restless days with Milton & twilight, her hazel
gaze far out the window
over April's brash hustle, motherly & perplexd, minding
                                my silence.
just syllables
cd make us touch
fingertips.
                        & her son waits also for her
when I arrive to wait for her, evenings
invading, will not

nod from his rockingchair, slight, 16 yrs old
& bright, bright, kind of a
mathematical wizard Jeanne whisperd/
                              chaos of citysounds up
from that 14th st subway stop one flight below is all there is between us,
        uttering no word in the dark.
& I can neither speak nor fear not to ache to hold me to his like a,
father.

            together, Solomon, this way, we wait
for her. while whatever harmony or song has wrencht me here, to yr
grim hurt, you hate, & hate
this yr first lonely place in my song where Jeanne my muse yr mother
leans smiling down to you/
            & she kisses yr hair

            cd shed rage
            shd love come.

or do I sing it wrong, Jeanne, when will I sing it right?
all of it effortful: how I break away; how I disappear;
how I vanish; how I abandon you; forget you; fall

mute as these long summer hours we spend wordless, motionless,
each of us in wonderment, how to heal, how to mend
what no one has severd yet
                what no one has broken.

what no one has severd yet
                        what no one has broken.

what no one has severd yet, & what no one has broken—

I wd sing about—. but how my song
                        stops.

Aphroditos Phalanthos, come from the sea. come here to me.

Jeanne, Jeanne, why is my song of you dying, Jeanne,
        do our bodies betray us
        do they yield us bleak measure
        mock exultations, or violate shockingly
        faith-hummed litanies of union, or

by my window, Jeanne, yr reluctant thin body, moonlit,
& the blue elms asleep beyond it in the courtyard, or

> in pigeon-fluttering noon, on Bleecker,
> yr hands fly sudden to yr mouth to stifle
> some injurd ideal of the loneliness returning

> or Brian, in wrencht
convolutions of the emblem—Brian-Jeanne—also
afraid, unbuttoning his child-shirt a child-day, this
ritual not passion, as my words come halting, remorseful,
unwillingly to bed with me, his blond slow arms
> aching not to embrace these
memories of—how shd I name them, Phalanthos?—

> freshborn innocent songs
> left to cough & cry on a mountain?

& I wd sing about—. but my song
> stops.

Aphroditos Phalanthos, come from the sea. come here to me.

& Charles, warm old friend, calls—you ought to go on with it, even
> so wounded a thing
& Bill calls—my friend Bill a poet—a tenderness
is in it. get on with it
Steve calls. I rail at my friend against my prison
Harry calls—Harry my friend a poet—aint the song
finisht yet, may I come for a visit?
& Juan calls—my friend Juan a poet—I must go to Spain
> I must go to Mexico
> I must find my lost father in the Philippines
> I must learn Spanish, I must search
> all my life I've tried to be *white*washt!
> my country's my prison, I must escape!

> *cd shed rage*
> *cd shed rage.*

my skin's my prison my body makes these wrong
                                    songs here

          of Brian whose body's one prison
by my bedside, in ritual sweat, belt grippt, folded, fisted
          with this ember-sear to punish the music, burnt
from my chest to my navel, done against sweet strange breathings, who gets
          paid & gets
          gone, vanisht
under shudders of palm leaves black against an aged-gold sullen great moon.

but what of the song, I lamented, & what of the rapture?
          & Jeanne, astonisht,
her soft cool hands on my forehead:
                              you mourn only

the sacred robin moaning at twilight from his brief spring tree.

          & I start to cry. & she hushes me.
          o, who can put the music back in that tree?

                         cd shed rage
                         cd shed rage
                         cd shed rage

                         shd love come.

Aphroditos Absconditus

FOR KATE BRAVERMAN

forlorn in a severance rain from root,
then to slave austerely to wail down insanity into my singing rages
        pleading stop stop me enthralld
by avidyā's big boot death grum fugue death dry fountain death pig pouf
        turdblossom cringing anonymous slurp I
beg trappt braying hate me dont hate me this is my
        song, sourd in brutality & the acrid stench of.
        pale sweated eye-
brows strong Lion transfixing me: growling slamming home bosst dim citizen this
        busted vainglorious maleficent fugitive choke-fuck.
& Lion he rears fierce in me somebody watch watch us a steely true blue
badgd snig maybe   & divine right Lion he roars suck & I wail my
        whole song down clear to my snuff-flick lone
some getting off grand last passions over my long dead tongue my own Lion & my
                                            [own brutish law.

        forlorn in a severance weed from rain,
a god I am & mine own slave so far have I faked me repetitive cold
        arrests sully me fast, once
spread darks about me before I cd figure, & devouring afteraborts narrow
        awake knobbykneed paunchy grayhaird in scrub
        oaks, redfaced stumbling
dry path to dry creek bed to lurk a long naked kneeling morning hidden
        dastard under thick blackwillow in
        shitsong in self wallow I
beg you beat me let me swallow you & strict eyes of my Lion please search me how to kill.
        this furious beating beggd,
        judgd abject we go,
daredevil Lee & Lion tailgating, los feliz western la brea gardner, scatter my
        limits, boundspreadeagled, drunken, druggd, gaggd. home.

        sung from a festering chasm here from now, un-
willing to be redeemed by losses / this late drift of ashes sweet my burnt sky down,
        wounding me with youth & nescience, how I
suffer my shy scarrd gristle upgroveling / erect divine Lion laughing & binding me,
        & implore to be force
        fed earth
        worms defild quit quick of

dying yes & has me as he has me strappt tight to my bed on my back his
        fingers upthrust harsh nails gouge has me
screaming muffled under my gag blasts rock up loud, clamps
        canines on my writhing & his belt repeatedly
& repeatedly as his young golden kneecaps sting my frozen gray
        hands, slops vodka past my gag, icecubes
stufft into my nostrils helpless pale thongbound wrists struggle glad, carolling bloody.
revolution war bloody birth inside me trees crack cries in the night.
eroticized cynicism parcht godhead acacia whom the hot wind hurts.
I am not where I am, saith the mad Lord God.
where safest   lost my home,
& poetry upbraids me to these depths of my Godhead.
death simply to want safety, put a stop to it. more fire,
        pyre sweet,   raise me
wrench me wretched gasping red out of said unto thy song, Goddess,
        more fire,   pyre sweet,
who are other people
wind in acacia
        sun doors hidden
                who are other people
                        four tangerine-colored carnations, two white
                            & rhythm-no-dancing & dancing-no-rhythm
                                burnisht-copper Irish setter wd rather not be petted
                                    "I feel more of working in the blind" / pay
me back if you are able how will I smoke drive my car, eat. wind
in acacia. while the child's black puppy glassfed
        drags her dangling colon across my fresh spring grass, Goddess,
                more fire, pyre
                        sweet, & lift me as loss & ashes thru my blue sun breath door.

        wind in acacia.
elven wrinkled grinning, Greatgrandma Fair holds out her dead Irish arms to me.
I'm on my skates, Anacapa st. sidewalk, front of my aunt's house, in Santa Barbara.
        & I wd like to tell you what the sun felt then she felt cold.
I wd like to tell you what the moon felt like then he felt nothing & what can a song feel?
        spiders in the palmtrees. rattlers in the outhouse. something
        deep underneath the sidewalk when you put yr ear down. yeah.
poem, I drive without insurance for you I wash my socks for you I smoke to death.
mother dont die dont die I want to be near you as soon as I can, mother.
& poem, I am going to be to you what a man wd be to a man who wd love him: I swear.
        composed from a compost here from below,
grudgesgrunts-angstoinks-baby-creaming-on-anguish-stupord-&-

muscled-Lion-snarling-&-mauling-me song: hungry to
cry I'll keep quiet sir I'll keep
quiet sir but shrink me into my zeroing music of puncht-out rhythms of
white knuckles pummeling, chest, lips, pummeld, singing
I can keep quiet sir I can keep quiet sir, & passing out, & coming to to
no cant let him cant
do this, stop, stop me, avid for, enthralld by
big boot death grum fugue death, dry fountain to wake to
to that memory of him crumpling my poems up, rasping thru my gag to try to to
cry out but passing out, to wake to
to his lunatic stare above me sweat pouring down, my stomach knee-gouged, his fists
battering my breasts, & endless my smile, & ecstatic my
fall, passing out, for how long now, coming to, in silence, to no one, in
pain, ribs fracturd lodgd against lungs,
& to narrow this joy thru this glittering zero, to meet my vain first self
abandond deserted one hand still tied,
my poems everywhere scatterd, throat bruised, hammerd-in
song shut, halfway downstairs stumbling, panting wild to holler out my
front door wide open on the great confusion, must
've dragged me into the bathroom, weakened & begging for sleep, floor splosht, walls
splosht, vomit, diarrhea, sickening ambers, eyes steely true shockt blue in
mirrord face crazd hot, bloody but not
my face, not mine, or was it, or is it, teeth lips tongue glorying in Lion-tang
& relishing my angerd-for, ineluctable, down, come.
spiders in the palmtrees. rattlers in the outhouse. something
deep underneath the sidewalk when you put yr ear down. yeah.

Sothsegger Scry

FOR HOLLY PRADO

resuffering my journal of winter '64, callow
perplexities this second symbolling flower
blossoms to memorialize, whether it fold shut
or unwithering open out, or never in time
uncover any human crying
not alive yet & never embraced alive. sometimes
my Ginny is in it, evolving thru thralldoms inseeing & scrying,
prophesying seven years safe without confusion,
& sometimes someone calling himself Leland is in it, gathering
his fluttering lights into complex
patterns, magnifying intensities until they shatter.
up against it, in camera/on camera. irredeemable, no rare
frailest santarasa, no gentlest human high & my whole way inward dying/ where
did he fuck up how did he go
wrong, huh; as merciful the snow
buried their dark apartment where they feared
to touch & to dream & to sing from the gasping source. o,
sothsegger, sothsegger scry, snow
compassions from my sky on their mute small weird. & absolve them.

almondblonde bitter lost, hidden hurt city sucks dirt to her,
slush shit to her, sooty cruise
smut to her, swollen lonely sweater shy tight pale
brave curve of her, defiled on the I.R.T.
o Ginny, my Ginny,
defiant-jawed shoulders tensed makeup caked, eyes
front, brittle dreams final & early all dead-
set against toughness break-
down, dazed visions, occult scars
from her burning sojourns thru unbreathable fires a-
blaze in her last hope crystal,
scrying, bewildered,
cantaloupes, oranges, mildewed, rotting,
dark ceiling unswept, heavy cobwebs swaying, in
enchantment by sorrowing yarrow stalks, star
charts tarot deck ouija board scam channels unto grace & forgetting how
strongly she wept, what blindly she fled from, why one stark song she feared, o
sothsegger, sothsegger scry, snow

solace from my sky on her mute dim weird/ & absolve, absolve her.

shared, mean, low rent, shared
brownouts, & failures shared & those tender
sudden deteriorations of their distrust, gaps
in it, some laughter some wise
cracks, joints passed under lamentations of lady day, or else satie very sadly, he
leaning hard on her, so seeming true & teaching, commanding, go
easier on the eyeline dont scorch the pork
chops sweep the fucking crud out, take fonder
care of yr sick black dog, Ginny; she timid, she wild, casting
curious lame spells against her psyche to believe him, what's the
use of his hands on her use of his tongue in her use of his wrong
song in her dont want you to sleep here, please let me
sleep here, then sleep here, dont go, please, please, sleep here.
& to the piteous plaint of the mad outlaw declaring
benign acts of aggression on an unknown poetry, they did kiss & they did suck,
& they interlock upon the bed, & on the floor, & up against the sill, biting,
huffing, & forct their dead false song as their dead truth leered. o,
sothsegger, sothsegger scry, snow
grieving from my sky on their lewd shared weird. & absolve them.

of Ginny, troubled, of
bewilderment his prophetess, in
dubiety uneasily, at noon & by candlelight,
trembling, scrying
imageries of neverwill as he watched her, terrified,
with sickness devouring his vision
& sickness oppressing his tongue,
unformed, isolate, in guilt of hid severance,
innocent of joy, escaping her,
fleeing into his future as he wrote it, into wept-for abysses,
svetaketu, plotinus, areopagite of the stammered nonnothing,
until a childhood arose in his throat & his blue sun breath door yielded
& his god of the bitter rasas descended to inseed him/ & he awoke.
as solstice dawn-neared, he cried,
self-moved, prophesying, his own vain seer,
of blind eyes, solitude, white serpents,
while beside him distant she listened to her lone stark song, & feared. o,
sothsegger, sothsegger scry, snow
consternations from my sky on his safe, cold weird/ & absolve, absolve him.

of Leland his
fraudulence, in shame of his meannesses, I
shiver thru this his journal of winter '64, these
shallow self-messages, scribbled
garbled vanities, these
hoarded-up passages in vomited self-desire, naked,
entangled in falsities,
christened his gloom autonomous, frightened, secret, closed,
cloistered his song from her occult presages, & brooded aloof from her;
as Ginny, wondering, scried for him,
divined grim full diaries for sorrow,
or whispered of
seven profound orbits thru holiness allotted him/ & he mocked her.
foresaw more than he cd dream to/ & he feared her. dared
deride her to embitterments, & broke her. dared
confound her to contradiction; mocked her. dared
enfold her & console her, in their darkness, where they cried.   o,
sothsegger, sothsegger scry, snow
gentleness from my sky on their wounding, wounded   weird. & absolve them.

yet not alive, never embraced alive, & his words, haunted,
indelible to recall it: stony, immobile, unflinching,
stubborn under his sudden yelled curses as he leaped at her,
out of his suffocated child uncontrollable, bursting, table up
ended radio exploded dinnerplates smasht lamps totaled
coffee cups splintered, blood-wet tomatoes burnt pork chops splattered, sliding
greasily down her scarified wall—& his chokt harsh fist, impotent, slasht,
gasht repeatedly against her shoulder, while
Ginny, my Ginny, neither cried out, nor stirred. & he fled,
orpheus of fraudulence prideblind under snowfall/ & she stared,
in her thralldom to her crystal where his phantom appeared,
singing their lone stark song, in vain. where-
ever in this his painstaking, resuffered, rhyme-enforct world,
faithful to the snowflake, solicitous of
ice, did he go wrong, huh; as merciless this rain
laments the bedarkened apartment of someone who feared
to touch & to dream & to sing from the gasping source, o
sothsegger, sothsegger scry, snow
astonishments from my sky on his feelingless weird/ & absolve me, absolve

absolve me.

Blackwillow Daybreak

FOR STEVEN ANTER

unguided ungratified unillumined unslept
untoucht stunted passions debauch brutish down to daybreak
anywhere anyone   quick men   dead men   my nameless
city park dirt path spring lust fog
agitating largo out of Ferndell/ how I
        grasp myself priest in grum hickmaning dawn
self-addicted grave groyne sweat, this
habit fatidic withal, mine ascetic my listless slug;
mine inburied ephemeral upanishad moon,
extinguisht, inflames it, delights it; how ungrowing I gasp
uphill toward blackwillow, hidden, shadowed
reborn fresh morning spring creekside bird-
sung proud paleblossomd owl-home wingd-ant-home snake-home, song-home, my
        kiss-the-ground sanctum blackwillow;
reach hilltop, stop,
breathe in in sharp hurt in clear sudden sight of it, crisp
piercing first light thru tentative fog lift,
early leaf cry, soft seed shimmer, moving, breathing, swaying
unto itself alone how no one shd deceive it,
shaking, yet no breeze to disturb it;
        & I wonder, & I see:
giant, muscled, hardond, stript
lunatic, writhing against treetrunk,
fragile seeds adrift in strange griefs around him,
fingertips on nipples, eyes half-closed, groaning,
watching my approach, not shifting his gaze away,
        dionysian long dark hair bejeweled yellowgreen,
young blackwillow leaves ensnard there, yellow blackwillow flowers fallen;
then in seedstorm under branches
shivering in my willowshell, spell-
bound, stunnd, how
wordless he sings to me, beckons to me, slave to his story, fierce
half-smile, shoulders, chest,
loins sweating pollenkisst/ his white torso,
harsh-breatht, archt against willow, his
thick thighs spread wide   & between them:
slender, living, stiff, low blackwillowlimb plungd-in upgouging,
        greast, abandond-to, ridden,
slid savaging grinding, crazd mean tight on,

thrashes his body back against dread, angrier, wilder,
& by his uprooted, panickt, uneartht outcry,
      begets this song,
anointed under showers of willowseed shaken downtrembling upon us.

on wet soil kneeling in my willowshell, near
broken giant breaking my husht seeds free, soon
to cease drifting over me   lost, ghost-human, kisses
earthkissing rhythm–tree, dresses, vanishes, fades from my story;
& my blackwillow song grown calm, solemn,
small birds, jays, bright blues, return,
my red ants up treetrunk, silver-wingd, flashing,
      how they signal my sunup;
sunbeams thru leaf-whispers onto low willowstub, glisten
of mucous, blood, sheer wings glint,
flying ants stumbling up phallus-staff, over
round-ridgd corona's blind eye, how
      insane in his half-light;
now, blackwillow, blackwillow, hide me,
for I unbuckle memory, for I undo my name;
for I strip me to childhood;
      for I slide down onto you
fingertips on nipples, my thighs spread wide,
for you pierce me, ravage me, for you make me cry loud;
for I beat my body back against dread; for these poor songs' pounding;
for shook blossoms scatterd meaningless from yr sky;
for I sob, for I gibber, for I babble crude psalm;
      for I desecrate;
for I sing ashamed of my daylight.

Yellowknife Bay

FOR DENNIS ELLMAN

under clouded noonsky, crossgraind, dry thunders muffled, whimper
of wind, last hours, Fort Providence, & hours-late bus, we wait
by hudson bay company, wooden porch steps, Slave
Indian children stare, frown, sullen-eyed; we board
mudcaked outback rattletrap, curses spat, dirtclods, rocks
flung after us; backfiring toward Yellowknife, Aussie
driver, Indian woman, two young Slave Indian men, Hank, me;
downpour again & overcast always; night; each riding silent, alone, & wind
whistling thru windowcracks; graveld highway, pitted;
swerve, slide, wheelslip; cold; impossible sleep;
lightning-lit poverties of villages, ancient tribes in their modern
                          squalor; word-road, pitchdark;
wilderness unanswering; no signs for me; my forest un-
                          yielding; word-rain, plainsong, pitchdark.

next day, Yellowknife New Town, mercenary, safe;
& bayward thru Old Town, quaint, & Latham Island bridge, Hank
leading; toward smoldering windborne garbage-stench, steep
downhill road where Dogbills die, warriors once,
slaveowners once, in their weatherd-dun box-huts by the dump;
last summer, drove ridge-route, L.A. to childhood, East
Bakersfield 2534 Lake Street not one bleakness changd, blight
amid blight; Indians; other poor; crossgraind oilsmoke sky; trees
dead; new boxes without frontyards, built on old frontyards,
memoried childscape crumbling behind them; no sidewalks, nothing
                          green; transfixt, pitchdark,
gazing; frontstoop roof, 2-x-4 proppt, on dad's mean shack, decrepit; look,
                          look, outhouse prison of pitchdark,
still standing; & I'm afraid; & my mother's afraid; fears
to be seen outdoors torn blue bathrobe flapping; suddenly
crying; why; why is she crying; in rain I see her; dark-haird,
wearing a blue bathrobe, standing still on planks that cover mud,
the way to the outhouse, in the storm, holding her
hands to her face, screaming, screaming; or I'm home from my canal, barefoot,
she's dressed-up, spitcurls auburn on her forehead, stands
on Lake Street with her suitcase; where are you going mommy;
o, sonny, she says, o, sonny, why did you come home so soon,
wait in the house, wait for yr father, & I stare thru the window,

179

taximan, taximan, sky getting pitchdark;
race down driveway, holler, taxi turns corner, holler, standing
rigid on Lake Street hollering in pitchdark;
now, Dogbills hammer-up stormwindows; under us,
volcanic outcroppings, glacier-groovd, Hank & I
stumble wind-deafend down boulders to Yellowknife Bay,
indigo pitchdark vast waterscape tempestuous in windsquall,
ice-stifled under snowfall soon;
breathstopping wingbeat terror-squawk raven-clash vicious above us,
beak-stab, blood-spray, feather-fall;
bleak plainsong sky over Great Slave Lake; unutterable omens
singing me home.

UNPUBLISHED TIRESIAS

for Gene Fowler: magic Tiresias song

Loving the juices of trees the tough Indian part
the deepest reflex struck from the world shoots out
    Dad mistaught me my sex while digging a deep home

for transplanting a young plum   he'd run away
from the farm   no trees there tall enough for him
    Now by shaman's song to be made to see how dim

my tough Indian part is   rayed forth from root
vision   Tiresias/vision: comes whatever your way
in form you form can form are or hope to be   I

say Tiresias greek is an Indian of the land our
feet fled from that you sing reach for be of Gene
new manbeast urging treesoul back to the sun.

Shape informs shape   snakesplitting stick struck
then can malewomb seeds to dance to treedrumbeat power
as you've sung my tongues back and it saps thru core

as mountains takes back Indian unto rock   juice of rock
deaths of a deathshape unbinding   Newbinding blind
Thebans come home at last with oracles   returned

quick for us at last where our feet are stuck unstuck
who purify the street   who make old land new of the loin
who plant back fathersblood pure under sod and rain

who shape with the snakestick   who dig the earth
who coil the meaning which makes the form   the breath
to father the fathers of the sun who sleep   who dream

    in the old clean soil of the brain.

[my doubletongues flame in my all-night extremitysucker]

my doubletongues flame in my all-night extremitysucker
        frightened of going, staying, coming,
I have moved forward. I have made progress the
        dam is damaged. disaster. nothing
follows order anymore. grizzled sorcerer in a split bikini
puffing round the lake everything flapping, nothing
        magic showing.
last night tonight tomorrow night.
lazing round the bend the muffler fell off I can hear myself cursing.
        whenever will this prick hurt good.

LATE POEMS

Annotation For That Which Follows

Terror outcast young girl trembling auburn soft pageboy fear blown
        tears, scream;
tiresian purloin san juan de la cruz cruise text cross out
        graphemes for
god outhouse captivity cry let me out cry poisoned defeated
        brutal, lewd;
despumate desquamate perineal bubo mary janes slap
        sharp upon
pavement his dislocalized speech immobilized arm her
        elbow skin
withered nervously recounting it ladder to which de
        lusional com
parison "wrongd ever rung of" bad catch
        me bad hurt

me bad hate me mama at

        orisonned out
set immiserizations mandala his
        mandatory sen
tencings fiery in child dreamt burnt flesh bloodtaste cess
        pool out
fall, writ, chalkt up in a shit shed shoeheel bang bars keep
        death row a
wake mandala aflame uncharred vermilion-haired satanhead in't whose
        blond eye
lasht boyhood bloodied boymate fled, sobbing under obscure care here in
        tensive care
here arroyos aflood in downcaster plain in purgative night in
        ebriate ca
rotid catheter celebrant rectal esophageal capillary-rain brainsbust in out

        burst

verse here; panning gold death valley; she grammardays 19two3 spring so
        lazily over
comix page age 7 quite contrary mary mary late on yr way to school a

       lone a lone
ly man's candies small movies stop pitchblack in secret by se
       cret ladder dis
guised "brought groceries in stood wide-eyes staring at
       nothing saw
right off the bat he couldn't move speak braced him from
       falling got him
into a chair called the" planets stars progeny of
       thunder cross
out thunder dim out kitchen railroad free
       way din in

gasp struck blank still

       'd space in
haled commere lemme showya a chokehold bud
       dy pale lasht
trust on summerstreet; whose lyric breeze whose parted locks
       what wounding sus
pends tender text in oblivion howsomever begrudging denials for
       given sick
nightwatcht breathings gone limp slippt grasp fallen knockt-out for
       real his
monkeymug kisst asphalt come-to ahowling, hands to his broke face stum
       bling home
but a stiffneckt brutish boy gets led by a god down planks in a mudwrackt yard gets
       turd-housed gets
lockt in in dank to unlearn in shiver in crumple in whimper let me out

       in out let me

out cloyed anguishes sweetrots his candies halt our schoolgirl in terri
       fied husht
mary jane shoes thin kneesocks frail pinafore tremulous instanter to
       flee she
screams eludes him kickt demonic out of her womb by his crude grum god
       who smasht his
sucking bottle in his mama's face blent splendor for his first gaze blood

                milk stream
ing noxious child vengeances boxed unto horrors hys
                terical cack
ling thru peckerwood flats san quentin sordors death
                row night
long longings to be gone to be scattered
                in isolate
sierra on the strong somber trees

                or wrencht in squal
id sleeps guided by a cross-eyed bald de
                mented bitch
past sabretootht text toward stone deaf stone
                eyed stone
tongued weavers of inflictions drencht under stone
                aged river of
avidyā scared little girl breathless to be safe near an oak
                tree by storm
fenced schoolyard whenas oak hides terror with his hideous smile his
                idiot out
stretcht arms panickt she runs screaming runs years reclines no tender
                text maker his
face in his maker's chest kisst where he slumbers dusk at window

                screen un

veils thick-scabbed visage forehead to chin seept pus glistens no hand a
                sleep ca
resses his neck no harsht sentencing suspended metastasis liver to
                lungs no
amorous breeze aroused among cedars; luger-rounds steept long in
                godhead of
stray cats strangled set fire to drowned, trusst dogs airgunned im
                paled on a
mopstick godhead of a thousand times stabbed prim pig vic
                torious man
slaughter laughter teen-aged caged kangaroo gang raped
                twice shank

slasht wrists pubescent laughter after last rippt-off mus
     tang never to

hang for a yellow-gut

     godhead in
scriptures bullets in an infant's laughter bad catch
     me bad hurt
me bad hate me mama "man I sure did blast those dumb punks'
     brains all
over the trees"—gentle abandoned childish text, silvery wet,
     outstrung in
awe struck leaves—

[1982]

[includes biographical notes on the life of Robert Alton Harris, currently
on Death Row ("Peckerwood Flats") at San Quentin; St. John of the
Cross, *Dark Night of the Soul*, translated and edited by E. Allison Peers]

He Who Delights in Signs

tilphussa without to drink thee
both tilphussa within

as when suckt about poet into poem's
more ruin in flame my deathmost

tilphussa of his goddess's juices
as of her serpent's tongue in my ears a
tiresian upwelling voracious not yet gone luminous down on honest as early as
sign as down on a
child's rift, rift of her portions fresh in
face eyes throat seeping arroyos make shift at,
threshold, as he who delights in signs as ascend from my glistening
madre, thru my well of her startlings, tilphussa,
in downcaster plain, at alphabet close, in cringing, in hiding
as in goddessskin of his herness her godskin who am

angerly glad flung, mad by infected
feastings, starkt as to dread, dasht to last
wishes, cobwebby viral word blood temblor this
stumbler in naked elision, enjambments stunned, at alarm's
distance, syllable hell in a panic deathwell toxic bittersweet sleep of who drink
thee

signs,   blinded in me as my astonied daughter
born dimmed as my manto,   gorgeously wounded
infant her gaze in-where on nowhere, scried sign severely,
as of her tendermost plaintext retting.
                              some god's doing.
                                        one of my grim kind.

      (blue sun breath door
      at tilphussa spring
      to drink so to die of, sexual of
ice gust bone clean vastation deathathenamymadre her potion.

has flayed me him child
hid hem of her robe

as fled tiresian thebic ills
blind beguttering gules flood

has forced me him cruelled
impelled marred future

flung scarred against signed
as hard breath self writing

death hard signed harder
as alone to go in

as in long to be gone
as together to be scattered or

long not to

[1984-1985]

[Tilphussa, or Telphousa: spring near Sphinx Mountain, from which
Tiresias prophesied he would drink and then die]

"When you put yr ear down":
Leland Hickman's Complete Poems

BY BILL MOHR

In devoting myself to cultural work as a small press editor and publisher for over a decade and a half in the 1970s and 1980s, I had the honor and good fortune to publish poets living throughout the United States, such as Alicia Ostriker in New Jersey, Len Roberts in Pennsylvania, and Jim Moore in Minnesota. Running a small independent literary venture in Southern California required more than an average degree of bravura, however, so while I was always alert to poets elsewhere, no doubt the companionship of the many quirky, maverick poets living in Los Angeles at that time helped sustain a venture that began with very little cultural capital, let alone the monetary version. Of all these poets, however, the one for whom I retain the largest measure of editorial affection and undiminished loyalty is, without doubt, Leland Hickman; it is no exaggeration to say that all of the poets I published owe a direct debt to Hickman, for it was primarily my immediate admiration upon reading some opening sections of "Tiresias" in 1972 that spurred me on to establish a publishing venture. I'm not certain what muse in the early 1970s informed me that the book-length publication of any portion of "Tiresias" in Hickman's lifetime would depend completely on my upstart project, but I do know that my major purpose in establishing Momentum Press was not only to bring attention to his astonishing poetry, but to embed it within a context of other poets whose contumacious poetics would provide a sympathetically interstitial community to bolster its distinction.

Hickman knew the vast majority of the poets in Los Angeles whose books I published or whose poems I anthologized. He, too, published many of them in a series of magazines he edited in Los Angeles over a period of a dozen years. Almost twenty years after his death in 1991, a huge swath of other innovative and often audacious poets across the country—only a small percentage of whom could be classified as Language writers—still recollect Lee Hickman's editorial projects with admiration, but a wider acknowledgment of his poetry lags far behind. One major impediment is that for close to twenty years it has been consigned to what Alaister Fowler has termed the "potential" canon; the only way prior to this book to encounter Lee Hickman's poetry was to launch a determined search of rare book catalogues in hopes of acquiring a pair of books containing the bulk of his published work. Unfortunately, having access to his poetry did not mean a reader would be able to appreciate the subtle rhythmic power and modulations in tempo and timbre of his incomplete long poem, "Tiresias," all of which would have been all too easily lost or diffused as a reader shifted back and forth between its bifurcation in *Great Slave Lake Suite* (1980) and *Lee Sr Falls to the Floor* (1991).

Great Slave Lake Suite, Hickman's only book to be published in his lifetime, contained all of section I:9:B of "Tiresias," as well as ten poems entitled "Elements," which in themselves constitute a distinct sequence, a long poem cantilevered out from a long poem. The *Suite* intermingles a long narrative about Hickman's adolescent desolation with meditations prompted years later by the redemptive yearning of his journey to a remote region in Canada. In addition to his early poems, Hickman's posthumous collection, *Lee Sr Falls to the Floor,* featured sections one through part A of section nine of "Tiresias," and its final installments. To be able to read, and re-read, "Tiresias" as a continuous text will provide a new generation of readers and poets with the means to appreciate the labyrinthine vibrancy of Hickman's lyricism.[1]

Leland Hickman was born on September 15, 1934 in Santa Barbara, California, but his family moved to East Bakersfield three years later, and stayed there throughout World War II. Childhood images of dispiriting poverty flicker throughout "Tiresias," and his upbringing was apparently marred by his father's ineptitude in providing much more than minimal sustenance. Hickman's sexual awareness and proclivity for vulnerable transgression seem to have started as early as age six; his interest in poetry was at least in part connected with these foreshadowings of his future topics. In one of his contributor's notes, he recounted that he "wrote his first poem in the sixth grade to impress (and I did!) a handsome male student teacher I was just nuts about."[2] In high school Hickman was one of the editors of the student newspaper, but he also became sexually involved with several older men, at least one of whom was sent to prison. Hickman himself spent time in a juvenile hall in 1948, an experience that according to his notes he intended to write about as the subject of part ten of Book One of "Tiresias." After graduating from high school, Hickman first attended college at the University of California, Santa Barbara, but transferred to the UC Berkeley in 1954, and was enrolled there through 1956. He published his first poem in *Occident* in 1955. He dropped out of college, and briefly visited New York City, then served in the army in 1957, stationed at Fort Ord.[3]

After his discharge from the army, he joined the Bishop's Company, and acted in their national tour in 1957, but was fired from the company for "getting potted in a church."[4] He spent the next three years in New York City and garnered some acting work in summer stock theater in Fulton, Ohio, in 1958.[5] He moved to Los Angeles in the early 1960s, and lived on Sunset Boulevard,

Santa Monica Boulevard, and a rooming-house at McCadden Place and Selma. The grimness of his first sojourn in Los Angeles adheres to the mournful lyricism of "O Blue Temple."

Hickman returned to New York City in 1963, and became involved with the off-off-Broadway scene, which included the Judson Poet's Theater, Theatre Genesis, Café Cino and Café La Mama. Hickman acted in a play by David Starkweather called "Who's Afraid of Virginia Woolf?" at Café Cino in 1964.[6] The main actress in that production, Lucy Silvay, also played the lead in a play by William Hoffman, which Hickman directed at Café La Mama. He also began studying acting under Frank Corsaro. Hickman once mentioned to me that, in response to an acting assignment, he had performed scenes from his life at the Corsaro's Acting Studio; the reaction had been one of two extremes: his fellow actors either loved or hated his autobiographical recreation.[7]

At the age of 30, Hickman began a serious effort to focus on poetry, but the tormented sexual ambivalence of his romantic liaisons complicated the process. "What does it mean," he asked himself in a short prose recollection, that "the period during which I most seriously struggled to discover if I had viable talent as a poet was also the period during which I lived with Ginny while at the same time visiting each day and/or night the 86 Street Subway . . . at the end of which I got arrested."[8] The relationship with the "soothsegger" Ginny ended after a violent argument, and a fierce altercation also marked the conclusion of an intense affair between Hickman and a bisexual actress with whom he lived for a brief time. Hickman's reference to being arrested for solicitation was the third such instance in New York City: the first occurred sometime in 1958-1959, and the second in 1963. Each time he was sentenced to a jail term.[9]

By November, 1965, he was living by himself at 306 E. 6th Street: "pretty much just walls and drafty floor. And a cat. And out of this solitude when I get the chance I'm apt to write poems and pretty bad letters, in which I suppose I make too much of what insightful types just shrug off."[10] Despite his pessimistic self-assessment, he had begun to send work out and to get it accepted in both New York (*Manhattan Review*) and Los Angeles (*Trace*). He had not yet completely turned away from theater. He was still attending classes at Corsaro's studio. One of the other students was Harry Northup, a young actor who had moved from Nebraska to New York City in 1963, and who eventually became one of Hickman's most loyal friends. In early December, 1965, Hickman invited Northup over to his apartment to rehearse a scene. By his own admission, Northup "never was into poetry" until he took home and assiduously read a copy of Donald Allen's anthology which Hickman lent him from "a whole bookcase full of poetry books."[11]

The death of Hickman's father from carbon monoxide poisoning on December 4, 1960 eventually became the subject of his first poem to achieve any widespread recognition. "Lee Sr Falls to the Floor" appeared in the Winter, 1966-1967 issue of *The Hudson Review*, and was then selected for an anthology supported by the National Endowment for the Arts. As part of this honor, Hickman received a $500 prize, which was certainly an encouraging award, but hardly the equivalent of the NEA's creative writing fellowships, for which he applied several times in the 1970s, only to be consistently rejected.[12]

Hickman began writing "Tiresias" in 1966 in New York City, and the first several poems (I:1 through I:8A and I:8B) appear to have been composed with new-found confidence. Section I:9:A, however, was not written until 1969. Although Richard Howard accepted two sections for *New American Review*, Hickman's straightforward accounts of his youthful promiscuity quickly exceeded the self-censorship limits that most editors in the United States acquiesced to, and it was not until he settled in Los Angeles that he began to meet editors who were willing to encourage his work on "Tiresias." The instigating motive for Hickman's decision to leave New York in the late 1960s remains unknown. He does not appear to have developed many friends in the poetry communities on the East Coast. In a letter to Joanne Kyger, Hickman mentioned influences and inclinations more than personal attachments. He knew "one poet—William Hoffman. He also is a playwright—having a play in Europe now. He's pretty good. I like Ted Berrigan, and especially Gene Fowler on the Coast. My own urges are pretty much Duncan, Olson and Snyder."[13] Northup had moved to Los Angeles in March of 1968 to pursue a film career, and they lost touch with each other. Whatever the impetus, Hickman returned to the West Coast in 1969, living briefly in Los Angeles and San Francisco in 1969-1970. His decision to settle in Los Angeles may have been influenced by the exigencies of the career of his companion, Charles Macaulay, who acted in many movies and television shows, including *Perry Mason*. Professional engagements as an actor also included residential benefits. When I first met Hickman, he was living with Macaulay in a house owned by Raymond Burr, and indeed, Burr ended up making a generous donation to Hickman's magazine, *Temblor*.

In 1970, Hickman certainly could not have anticipated that Los Angeles would prove to be the most hospitable city for him to develop as a poet. The abundance of poetry magazines in Los Angeles in the 1950s had dwindled considerably by 1967, although a reviviscency was well underway by the time Hickman settled in Los Angeles for good. Perhaps the most important chance event in the early stages of Hickman's new life in Los Angeles happened when he spotted a newspaper announcement for a poetry reading at Beyond Baroque by Harry Northup and other members of the Venice Poetry Workshop. Hickman surprised Northup by showing up for the reading, and then began attending Beyond Baroque's Wednesday night workshop, which remains the longest running free poetry workshop on the West Coast. The workshop was led by John Harris, who would soon become the owner of Papa Bach Bookstore, and Joseph Hansen, whose David Brandstetter series of mystery novels featured the first openly gay detective in the genre. On Wednesday evenings, Hansen repeatedly enumerated the merits of Hickman's poem, "Lee Sr Falls to the Floor," as well as his work-in-progress to the workshop, which included poets such as Kate Braverman, Wanda Coleman and James Krusoe. By 1972, Hickman had started giving readings of sections of "Tiresias," including one to a packed house at Papa Bach Bookstore that featured the portion of I:9:B beginning "PAINT CHILD AT PAIN AT SHOCK AT."[14]

Hickman's acceptance as a poet in Los Angeles eventually led to an offer by John Harris to take over the position of poetry editor of *Bachy* magazine in 1978, and Harris was gratified enough with Hickman's work that he became the general editor and production manager of the magazine for its final half-dozen issues. Old habits revived themselves, however, and he was arrested again in 1974 and 1975 for having sex in Griffith Park. This renewal of his pattern of risky behavior was also accompanied by a writer's block that had started after he finished the long narrative section of 9:B, and it was not until September, 1975 that he broke through it with "The Hidden," a poem that once again addressed the death of his father. By the end of 1977, he had written three more of the poems that make up the "Elements."

A groundswell of anticipation for a book of his poems began to sweep away his debilitating doubts, and critical attention for his project accelerated after he served as the lead poet in my anthology, *The Streets Inside: Ten Los Angeles Poets.*[15] When *Great Slave Lake Suite* was published in 1980, and then nominated by the *Los Angeles Times* as one of the five best books of poetry for that year, few of Hickman's peers were surprised by the resounding praise his book received. Almost all of the book's reviews, including pieces written by David Clothier, Rudy Kikel, Stephen Kessler, Clayton Eshleman and Martin Nakell, acknowledged Hickman's powers as a poet to render in solemn music a catharsis of a life often given over to voluntary abjection.[16]

Despite the voluminous praise bestowed on *Great Slave Lake Suite*, the book sold poorly. Less than half of its print run of 1,000 copies sold within the first two years. I did take 50 unbound sets of sheets and produce a limited hardcover edition, which pleased him immensely, but after Hickman's attempts to attract a more mainstream publisher who would commit to publishing the entire work were rebuffed, he found himself struggling to write the next sections of Book I. His tenure as editor of *Bachy* magazine seemed to provide an immediately gratifying measure of power, which counterbalanced his own struggle to eke out a minimal living, and as he began to sense that the enthusiastic reviews of *Great Slave Lake Suite* were only an ironic adumbration of his future marginality as a poet, he increasingly sought solace in editing. When Papa Bach Bookstore stopped publishing *Bachy* in 1981, Hickman launched another magazine, *Boxcar*, with Paul Vangelisti, before starting his own magazine in 1985. Hickman is best remembered as the editor of *Temblor* magazine, which terminated with its tenth issue in 1989 after the onset of his illness with AIDS.[17] His devotion to poets who contributed to a renewed patrimony of the avant-garde during the century's penultimate decade won him widespread admiration among communities and coteries dissatisfied with what Charles Bernstein has characterized as official verse culture. *Temblor* served as the meeting point for many poets whose work was featured in Ron Silliman's pivotal anthology, *In the American Tree*, as well as a considerable number of poets Hickman classified as maverick innovators. Although Hickman's own poetry wasn't associated with Language writing, he offered both those poets and others with sympathetic affinities a respectful haven.

Hickman's commitment to this editorial labor cost him dearly. In order to make a living, Hickman worked as a typesetter. One of his primary motivations in keeping the job was that it enabled him to do production work on the magazine in the late evening after he finished the day's job. At a conference at the University of California, San Diego, on feminist publishers and editors entitled "Page Mothers," Marjorie Perloff gave a talk in which she nominated Hickman as an honorary "page mother," and at one point in the talk, her voice reached a tone of incredulity: "How did he do it?" she wondered.[18] The answer to that question has to grapple with not only the enormous personal sacrifices he made, but must also account for how he managed to overcome memories of personal deprivation he endured as a child in doing so. The improbable personal transformation into a selfless editor remains a harrowing accomplishment that underpins this collection of poetry.

As important and valuable as Hickman's editorial work was, the time has come for his curatorial accomplishments to accept a secondary designation, and for his poetry to have its turn. The challenges facing the readers of this book include the need to work through the poem several times simply to gain a basic understanding of the poem's structure. The organization of "Tiresias" is far more complex than a Fibonacci sequence. Although Hickman would probably be disappointed in me for suggesting the following strategy as a way of easing into the poem, I will make it anyway. New readers might be best off in first reading the "Elements" several times each, both individually and then as a sequence. For those readers weaned on a poetics of "first reading, best reading," I'm afraid there is no way around it: in order to speak of this poem, the reader of "Tiresias" must approach it the way a classical musician would approach her or his attempt to master a Rachmaninoff piano piece. The poem must be rehearsed until finger memory is achieved. I would encourage the reading strategy of starting with the "Elements" because they can be experienced as separate, discrete poems. Because each of the ten "Elements" has a distinct emotional theme, in fact, they are more likely to be selected as representative writing in future anthologies.

But as part of the autobiographical collage of Hickman's journey, the "Elements" were destined by Hickman to be woven into part B of the ninth section of the first book of "Tiresias." As an initial note of guidance, then, we should turn to Hickman's own description: "I always intended them to be a complete piece, but I had no idea in advance how the thing was going to look. I didn't write the elements knowing where they were going to fit when they were rewoven, or intertwined with the other elements. That was a process of trial and error—I put them together in several different ways."[19] The tentative arrangement and rearrangement of the "Elements" within *Great Slave Lake Suite* is the method by which Hickman pushed away from the kind of narrative overdetermination associated with the confessional school, which "Tiresias" could be consigned to on a superficial level. Hickman, though, insisted on a distinction between his work and the confessional school: "One reviewer said I'm writing at the end of a long line of confessional poets—And I don't know what that means. I don't know what they mean when they say *confessional*. So I think they're pointing at sexuality, or the confession of so-called shameful things. Robert Lowell said people shouldn't be angry at us for that, because we don't really confess anything shameful. But my poem could be looked at that way because I *am*. There's a lot of sexuality in the poem. It's absolutely necessary to the poem. Sexuality is a metaphor for many other things in the poem, and it's autobiographical, it's very much a part of my life, about being gay in America at a certain social and economic level at a time when it was very difficult to be gay in America, and how living in that repression formed me.

"It's not important the meaning be the same as my life, or as I would envision my life. If I sat down and wrote an event, trying to impose an interpretation on it, I wouldn't be making a poem. I wouldn't be discovering anything.

And so I do things to fool myself, by doing material backwards, so to speak, then putting it together later. Not knowing how it's going to fall together, what it's going to say, I discover incredible things. When I was in therapy I found as I went along that I had already written all of it out in the poem. Just hadn't recognized it on the level a therapist tries to make you recognize those things. Now I read the poem seeing it telling *me* things."[20]

For readers who find their first encounter with some of the "Elements" too daunting, I would encourage them to read "Lee Sr Falls to the Floor," and then to read "The Hidden," which "re-runs" that poem through a more formal structure. Interestingly enough, although many critics praised the *Suite*, none discussed the form of "The Hidden," and the absence of even this basic description suggests the sketchy, even if well intended, level of critical attention Hickman's work has received. "The Hidden" is twelve stanzas long, with the first stanza containing nine lines. An observant reader will notice that Hickman increases the number of lines in each subsequent stanza until the seventh stanza is fifteen lines long; the stanza length then decreases one line per stanza until the final stanza, which has ten lines. The form of the poem falls short of completing an oval of ripening grief and incremental reconciliation, and leaves a subsiding vacancy at the end, as if to insist that no final resolution or closure can be attained.

I once asked Hickman why he had picked the Great Slave Lake in Canada as a place to travel to and to use as the setting for his poem. He said that he had wanted to go there ever since he had seen it on a map when he was a child. If one looks at a detailed depiction of western Canada, one can see the names of places associated with specific poems: Fort Providence, Yellowknife Bay. One prominent place at the lake is not included in the titles of the "Elements," however: Fort Resolution. Hickman told me that his visit did not include that town, and perhaps the literal journey foreshadowed the unfinished cycle of his writing. The publication of this collection of his work represents a resolution of sorts, or at least an embodiment of a vision that exudes a willingness to risk all for the sake of an irrefutable leap across a chasm. In all of its vatic ripeness, "Tiresias" pauses here in this book, waiting for you to listen closely.

> spiders in the palmtrees, rattlers in the outhouse. something
> deep underneath the sidewalk when you put yr ear down. yeah.[21]

August, 2008
Long Beach, California

Notes

[1] Since I am not an impartial commentator, I would be remiss in not acknowledging from the start more specific details of my long and sometimes turbulent friendship with Leland Hickman, which began with my selection of the five opening poems of "Tiresias" for the second issue of *Bachy*, a literary magazine published by Papa Bach Bookstore in Los Angeles for ten years (1972-1981). I started my own magazine, *Momentum*, in 1974, and included selections of "Tiresias" in four issues, as well as close to thirty pages of entirely different sections in two anthologies of Los Angeles poets, *The Streets Inside* and *Poetry Loves Poetry*. Hickman served as a mentor to me in my earliest years as a poet, and made useful editorial suggestions about my selections for the first two issues of *Momentum*. I began publishing books in 1975; no matter what doubts Hickman may have had about his writing, he always knew that I had complete faith in his talent and vision as an artist and that I would be there for him as a publisher. I should add that I gave him a free hand as to what poems would constitute a manuscript.

[2] *The Streets Inside: Ten Los Angeles Poets* (Santa Monica, CA: Momentum Press, 1978), 2.

[3] Hickman recorded a list of his addresses from birth to the early 1970s, a copy of which is in his archives at the University of California, San Diego. My thanks to Stephen Motika for finding this list as well as several other relevant fragments of biographical material during a joint visit to his archive in February, 2008.

[4] Hickman. Letter to Joanne Kyger, December, 1965. Hickman archive, UCSD.

[5] Hickman. Unpublished, single-spaced three-page prose fragment. This piece of autobiographical reflection seems to have been an attempt to address underlying questions about the personal relationships examined in "Aphroditus Absconditus."

[6] "Notes on Aphroditus Absconditus." Although Hickman seems to have had only this one acting role at Café Cino, one should not underestimate the larger significance of this intersection of a young poet with artistic experimentation and cultural change. Café Cino was known as the off-off-Broadway venue that was the most open to work by gay playwrights about gay subjects.

[7] Hickman's fondness for the theater and performance occasionally surfaced even after he decided to devote his life to poetry. Dennis Phillips has often spoken of an astonishing evening in which Hickman showed up at a class he was teaching at the Art Center in Pasadena, and performed Shakespeare's *Henry V*. Shortly after Hickman died, I had dinner with Charles Macaulay, and he told me that a friend had reported mentioning Hickman's death to another acquaintance, whose first ascertainment was to inquire, "You mean Lee Hickman the actor?"

[8] "Notes on Aphroditus Absconditus." Hickman interrogates himself with this question in the opening sentence.

[9] List of chronological addresses. Hickman also wrote a short prose self-reflection about the experience of being arrested after his sixth arrest in 1977. In this commentary, Hickman says that he will not tell anyone about it, but he did use the occasion of an interview with John Rechy to discuss the trauma of this juridical interdiction. Hickman also discusses the influence of Rechy's writing on his poetry. *Bachy: A Journal of the Arts in Los Angeles*, No 17, Spring, 1980. "The Relentless Pursuit of Integrity," an interview with John Rechy, pages 3-11.

[10] Letter to Joanne Kyger.

[11] Leland Hickman. Interview with Harry Northup. *Bachy* 11, 1978, page 5. A comment by Northup during the interview ("I feel more of working in the blind") appears in *Great Slave Lake Suite*, along with a series of comments or images from other interviews with Holly Prado, Deena Metzger, James Krusoe and myself. Northup, in turn, quoted Hickman about his arrest in Griffith Park in a poem Northup wrote for the title poem of his collection, *Enough the Great Running Chapel*. One quick approximation of Hickman's skill as a typesetter is that he typeset Northup's 250-page book in about 12 hours at NewComp Graphics Center at Beyond Baroque, and made a total of less than a dozen errors. A couple years after he died, I met a typesetter who had worked with him. "We gave him the difficult jobs," she said.

[12] The three poetry judges were Robert Duncan, Anne Sexton, and Louis Simpson, and the preliminary readers included Ron Padgett, Lewis Warsh, and Dick Gallup. Over 350 different magazines submitted several issues each for consideration, and how Hickman's poem survived the winnowing is unknown. In a four-page preface to the volume, the second in a series which was terminated after number three, George Plimpton and Peter Ardery noted that "each poetry judge was asked to make a specified number of selections to go directly into the volume" (viii).

[13] Letter to Joanne Kyger.

[14] Hickman wrote about the reading as a moment in which he received unconditional support for his poem. It had an extraordinary impact on the audience, which included a young book clerk at Papa Bach named William ("Koki") Iwamoto, who until he encountered Hickman's poetry had primarily been interested in the work of W.S. Merwin. Iwamoto went on to open his own bookstore, Chatterton's, on North Vermont Blvd. Chatterton's was known for its hospitality to Los Angeles poets and their magazines and books. Iwamoto paid for books up front, and sponsored many readings at his store. Not all of Hickman's readings, however, went as well as these bookstore appearances. In sharing a double-bill with Robert Peters at Beyond Baroque, Hickman read far longer than he should have, and Peters quite justifiably got tired of waiting for his second turn, and left in the middle of Hickman's performance. Dennis Ellman's poem, "After a Reading by Leland Hickman," which appeared in issue number five of *Momentum* magazine, is a memorable account of that incident. Peters went on to write two very enthusiastic reviews of Hickman's work, so the occasion did not prove detrimental to Hickman's career in the long run.

[15] Singling out Hickman's poems for special notice, Bob Peters and Stephen Kessler wrote two long reviews of the anthology, which Hickman ran in *Bachy* magazine in 1979. It should be noted, however, that it wasn't just Hickman whose writing was being recognized as indicative of a complex literary outburst in Southern California. Los Angeles poets, as an outsider group, were beginning to attract serious mainstream attention in their hometown. The late Robert Kirsch also reviewed the anthology in the Los Angeles Times, and accorded this new wave of poets the distinction of a "golden age." He also commented that the poets were difficult to classify: call them "no-school," which was an accurate characterization of the maverick poets in Los Angeles at that time. A quick census of its most prominent figures working in Los Angeles at time would have to include Holly Prado, Wanda Coleman, Paul Vangelisti, Charles Bukowski, Steve Richmond, Harry Northup, Kate Braverman, James Krusoe, Eloise Klein Healy, Don Gordon, Bert Meyers, William Pillin, Gerald Locklin, Jack Grapes, Elliot Fried, Manazar, John Thomas, Robert Crosson, K. Curtis Lyle, Joseph Hansen, John Harris, Alvaro Cardona-Hine, Doren Robbins, Ameen Alwan, Deena Metzger, Dennis Phillips, Peter Levitt, Martha (Lifson) Ronk, Ron Koertge, Marine Robert Warden, and Dennis Ellman. Youthful voices such as Dennis Cooper, Bob Flanagan, and Laurel Ann Bogen were also beginning to be noticed. The widespread skepticism that the Los Angeles poetry roster was primarily made up of acolytes of Charles Bukowski was rapidly being dispelled. *The Streets Inside* featured the work of the following poets in this order: Leland Hickman, James Krusoe, Holly Prado, Deena Metzger, Peter Levitt, William Mohr, Kate Ellen Braverman, Eloise Klein Healy, Harry Northup, and Dennis Ellman. A reading that celebrated the December, 1978 publication of the anthology was held at Lenny Durso's Intellectuals & Liars Bookstore in Santa Monica in early January, 1979.

[16] David Clothier's review appeared in a column he wrote for the Los Angeles Times Book Review. Also reviewed along with *Great Slave Lake Suite* were Louis Simpson's *Caviar at the Funeral* and the late Vicki Hearne's *Nervous Horses*. Clayton Eshleman's review was the lead item in Beyond Baroque's *Poetry News*, and Martin Nakell's review appeared in Eshleman's *Sulfur*. Rudy Kikel's review appeared in *Gay News*. Nakell became the publisher of Hickman's posthumous book.

[17] Lee Hickman died on May 19, 1991. As soon as Hickman died, Charles Macaulay called and asked me to write a statement to send to the newspapers. The obituary that appeared in the Los Angeles Times in May, 1991, was taken almost verbatim from what I faxed to the newspaper from my typesetting job at Radio & Records. I also faxed my summary of his life and accomplishments to the New York Times, which declined to notice his death.

[18] "Page Mothers," Cassette Tapes. Archive for New Poetry, UCSD.

[19] "An Obsession with Meaning: Lee Hickman's Life and Work" was a combination interview and review of *Great Slave Lake Suite* by Laurel Delp published in *L.A. Weekly*, Dec. 12-18, 1980, Vol.3, No. 2. Delp also included her interview with Hickman in a subsequent article, "The License to Write:

L.A. Poets Start a New Tradition of their Own," which appeared in *California Living Magazine* in the January 31, 1982 issue of the *Los Angeles Herald Examiner.*

[20] Ibid.

[21] *Great Slave Lake Suite, "Aphroditos Absconditus."*

LELAND HICKMAN was born on September 15, 1934, in Santa Barbara, California. He lived with his family in Bakersfield from 1937 to 1945 and on a farm in Carpinteria for one year before returning to Santa Barbara, where he attended high school. In addition to acting in high school plays, Hickman performed in local theater productions of the Children's Theatre of Santa Barbara and the Group L Theatre Workshop. Hickman attended Santa Barbara College, now University of California, Santa Barbara, and later studied at the University of California, Berkeley, where he played with the Berkeley Drama Guild.

After a tour in the Army, he moved to New York City to continue his career in theater. Hickman toured nationally with the Bishop's Company in 1957, worked in the Canal-Fulton Summer Theatre in Ohio in the summer of 1958, and performed with the Equity Library Theatre in New York City. He subsequently studied on scholarship at the New York Academy of the American Shakespeare Festival. In 1960, Hickman returned to California to play at the Equity Library Theatre West in Los Angeles. He remained in Los Angeles for three years, then moved back to New York. He returned to California in 1969, and after a short time in San Francisco, settled permanently in Los Angeles with his partner, the actor Charles Macaulay.

His literary career began in the middle 1960's with the publication of "Lee Sr Falls to the Floor" in *The Hudson Review*. A book-length section of his serial poem, "Tiresias," entitled *Tiresias I:9:B: Great Slave Lake Suite* was published by Momentum Press in 1980. It was named a finalist for the *Los Angeles Times* Book Award in Poetry. Although Hickman did not finish "Tiresias," additional portions were published in *Manhattan Review*, *Trace*, *Momentum*, *Bachy*, *New American Review*, *LA Weekly*, *Los Angeles Herald Examiner*, *Rara Avis*, *Little Caesar*, *Invisible City*, *Boxcar*, and the anthology *The Streets Inside: Ten Los Angeles Poets*. A second book, *Lee Sr Falls to the Floor*, which collected early poems and several sections of "Tiresias," was published posthumously by Jahbone Press in 1991.

Hickman worked as the poetry editor for the legendary Los Angeles literary magazine *Bachy*, published by Papa Bach Bookstore, from 1977 to the spring of 1981. He edited issues nine to eighteen. In 1981, he co-founded with Paul Vangelisti the magazine *Boxcar: A Magazine of the Arts*, which ran for two issues. In 1985, Hickman began editing and publishing *Temblor*, which continued for ten issues.

He died in Los Angeles of AIDS-related causes on May 12, 1991. He was 56.

NIGHTBOAT BOOKS, a nonprofit organization, seeks to develop audiences for writers whose work resists convention and transcends boundaries. We publish books rich with poignancy, intelligence, and risk. Please visit our website, www.nightboat.org, to learn more about us and how you can support our future publications.

The Lives of a Spirit/Glasstown: Where Something Got Broken
     by Fanny Howe

The Truant Lover by Juliet Patterson (Winner of the 2004 Nightboat
     Poetry Prize)

Radical Love: Five Novels by Fanny Howe

Glean by Joshua Kryah (Winner of the 2005 Nightboat Poetry Prize)

The Sorrow And The Fast Of It by Nathalie Stephens

Envelope of Night: Selected and Uncollected Poems, 1966-1990
     by Michael Burkard

In the Mode of Disappearance by Jonathan Weinert (Winner of the
     2006 Nightboat Poetry Prize)

Your Body Figured by Douglas A. Martin

Dura by Myung Mi Kim

The All-Purpose Magical Tent by Lytton Smith (Winner of the 2007
     Nightboat Poetry Prize)

Absence Where As (Claude Cahun and the Unopened Book) by
     Nathanaël (Nathalie Stephens)

Century of Clouds by Bruce Boone

FORTHCOMING TITLES

In the Function of External Circumstances by Edwin Torres

)((eco (lang)(uage(reader)) edited by Brenda Iijima

Poetic Intention by Édouard Glissant

A Tonalist by Laura Moriarty

Ghost Fargo by Paula Cisewski (Winner of the 2008 Nightboat
     Poetry Prize)

This book was made possible by a grant from the Topanga Fund, which is dedicated to promoting the arts and literature of California.

The following individuals have supported the publication of this book. We thank them for their generosity and commitment to the mission of Nightboat Books:

Charles Bernstein
Elizabeth Motika
Marjorie Perloff
Benjamin Taylor

In addition, this book has been made possible, in part, by a grant from the New York State Council on the Arts Literature Program.

NYSCA
New York State Council on the Arts